SpringerBriefs in Cybersecurity

Cybersecurity is a difficult and complex field. The technical, political and legal questions surrounding it are complicated, often stretching a spectrum of diverse technologies, varying legal bodies, different political ideas and responsibilities. Cybersecurity is intrinsically interdisciplinary, and most activities in one field immediately affect the others. Technologies and techniques, strategies and tactics, motives and ideologies, rules and laws, institutions and industries, power and money—all of these topics have a role to play in cybersecurity, and all of these are tightly interwoven.

The SpringerBriefs in Cybersecurity series is comprised of two types of briefs: topic- and country-specific briefs. Topic-specific briefs strive to provide a comprehensive coverage of the whole range of topics surrounding cybersecurity, combining whenever possible legal, ethical, social, political and technical issues. Authors with diverse backgrounds explain their motivation, their mindset, and their approach to the topic, to illuminate its theoretical foundations, the practical nuts and bolts and its past, present and future. Country-specific briefs cover national perceptions and strategies, with officials and national authorities explaining the background, the leading thoughts and interests behind the official statements, to foster a more informed international dialogue.

More information about this series at http://www.springer.com/series/10634

Philippe Baumard

Cybersecurity in France

Springer

Philippe Baumard
Conservatoire National des Arts et Métiers
Paris
France

and

School of Economic Warfare—ESLSCA
Paris
France

ISSN 2193-973X ISSN 2193-9748 (electronic)
SpringerBriefs in Cybersecurity
ISBN 978-3-319-54306-2 ISBN 978-3-319-54308-6 (eBook)
DOI 10.1007/978-3-319-54308-6

Library of Congress Control Number: 2017936344

Printed on acid-free paper

This Springer imprint is published by Springer Nature
The registered company is Springer International Publishing AG
The registered company address is: Gewerbestrasse 11, 6330 Cham, Switzerland

Foreword

France has always been at the forefront of technological developments in cybersecurity. Its base is in defense and aerospace and its paradigms guiding its sovereignty in security have provided the country with a unique perspective on cybersecurity, supported by great capacities. It started early with strategic thinking and industrial acquisitions in the field, with academic leadership and technology development. Yet France has also been somewhat closed to the outer world with its thoughts and concepts. To a large part, this was intentional. France did not want to share any of its evolution before it reached maturity and much of it was considered national only. Accordingly, most of the activities in aerospace and defense still have not surfaced.

Philippe Baumard has been a part of the history of the field and is an excellent scholar, providing both a first hand account of things and a very thorough, critical, and systematic analysis. This combination is what renders this insight into France so interesting and valuable. It not only opens a window into the mostly secluded activities in France, but also provides a coherent account of histories and causalities of rather universal relevance for any country concerned with strategic cybersecurity. From his accounts on the early history of hacking and IT-security in France, to his systematic analysis of persistent technical issues and the difficulties of possible responses to his political and economic analysis of the underlying issues, the present work provides explanations for many of the hidden and complex mechanisms of the field and develops heuristic frameworks to render them detectable and manageable in the future.

Without question, it will be a must-read for anyone concerned with or interested in the history of cybersecurity or cyberstrategy.

March 2017

Sandro Gaycken
ESMT Berlin

Contents

About the Author

Philippe Baumard, Ph.D. is the founder and CEO of Akheros, Inc., a Paris based machine learning cybersecurity laboratory, laureate of the 2013 and 2014 France national innovation awards. Dr. Baumard is Professor at the French National Conservatory for Arts and Manufacturing (CNAM), Paris; associate researcher at Ecole Polytechnique; and Professor, Dean for Research, at ESLSCA's School of Economic Warfare. He has been a visiting professor in leading universities such as Stanford, UC Berkeley, and New York University. Dr. Baumard has published key publications on cyber-warfare since as early as 1994, and is a renowned expert in the domain of information warfare and implicit learning. He authored 10 books and more than 90 refereed research articles.

Chapter 1
Introduction

Abstract This chapter gives a general overview of this monograph and provides an executive summary of its findings.

Keywords Informational crises · National cybersecurity strategies · Cybersecurity · Hacking · Information warfare · Cognitive warfare · Cyber-war · Cyber-defense

Modern informational crises have penetrated most societal arenas, from healthcare, politics, economics to the conduct of business and welfare. Stock markets are dependent upon a mass of information that clearly surpasses the human limitations of sensemaking, with or without the support of modern information technologies. Military operations intertwine with a global information infrastructure that leaves no place hidden from public scrutiny, no rationale unquestioned, no legitimacy freed of questioning. Dissymmetry of the weak defending against the incumbent makes an intensive use of deliberate information crises, aimed at challenging the rationale, the legitimacy and the morale of its offensives. One defensive mechanism, not unknown to nature and biological systems, is to develop information strategies that defy opponent's sensemaking, and hence creates a somatic state within its ranks. Such deliberate informational crises are called "asymmetric campaigning." As organizations are more and more dependent on information for the continuity and stability of their operations, they also become more vulnerable to cyber-destabilization, either genuine, or deliberate for the purpose of gaining geopolitical advantage, waging wars, conducting intellectual theft and a wide range of crimes.

Subsequently, the regulation of cyber-space has grown into an international effort where public, private and sovereign interests often collide. By analyzing the particular case of the French national strategy and capabilities, this monograph investigates the difficulty of obtaining a global agreement on the regulation of cyber-warfare. A review of the motives for disagreement between parties suggests that the current regulation framework is not adapted to the current technological change in the cybersecurity domain. Our monograph suggests a paradigm shift in

P. Baumard, *Cybersecurity in France*, SpringerBriefs in Cybersecurity,
DOI 10.1007/978-3-319-54308-6_1

handling and anchoring cyber-regulation into a new realm of behavioral and cognitive sciences, and their application to machine learning and cyber-defense.

National cybersecurity strategies (NCSS) greatly differ from a country to another, according to the role of information in their legal, historic, sociological and constitutional frameworks. In the early 1990s, the term only embraced the definition of a national strategy in the confined domain of computer security, limited to the usage of computer systems, networks, electronic capabilities in infrastructures, defense and civil protection. The global digitalization, which occurred in the late 1990s, dramatically increased the pervasiveness of information technologies in society: shaping opinions, defining cultural boundaries, transforming economies, defense systems and day-to-day life of the human species. In this evolution, the contemporary concept of *cybernetics* is closer to the holistic elaboration of Ampère in the XIXth century, than its mechanistic conceptualization of Wiener in 1948.

The French philosopher André-Marie Ampère first coined the word "*cybernétique*" in his 1834 essay: *Essai sur la philosophie des sciences.*[1] "Relentlessly", he wrote, a government "needs to chose between the most appropriate measures to achieve its goals" (p. 141). For Ampère, *cybernetics* is an "art of governing," which he qualifies as a "third order science," along with *diplomacy,* and *power theory* (Ibid., p. 143). In his 1948 book, *Cybernetics or control and Communication in the Animal and the Machine,* Norbert Wiener introduced the long-lasting analogy between computing machines and the nervous system; envisioning "numerical machines" (digital computers) as a founding stone of a self-organizing society.

The "cyber" prefix encompasses today both its early epistemology (Ampère, Wiener) and *anything* related to use of electronic and digital computation and communications in the conduct of national affairs. This causal ambiguity is at the source of many international tensions. Russia and the People Republic of China do not accept an enlarged definition of "cyber-security" that would contradicts some founding and not negotiable principles of their constitutions. This situation eventually led NATO to launch a special working group working on definitions.[2] The term "cyber-defense" has been made official in France by the 2008 national defense white paper (*Livre Blanc de la Défense*[3]). On pages 53 and 96, the report uses the term "cyber-space"[4] to designate European information systems; assuming that a "cyber-war" (p. 106) could trigger a kinetic and conventional conflict; and defining "*cybernétique*" as the fourth military domain after ground, air and maritime operations (p. 192). The same 2008 national defense White Paper enacts as a

[1]Full text available at: http://www.ampere.cnrs.fr/textes/essaiphilosophie/pdf/essaiphilosophiesciences_1.pdf.

[2]https://ccdcoe.org/cyber-definitions.html.

[3]http://www.ladocumentationfrancaise.fr/var/storage/rapports-publics/084000341.pdf.

[4]«Les moyens d'information et de communication sont devenus les systèmes nerveux de nos sociétés, sans lesquels elles ne peuvent plus fonctionner. Or le «cyberespace», constitue par le maillage de l'ensemble des réseaux, est radicalement différent de l'espace physique: sans frontière, évolutif, anonyme, l'identification certaine d'un agresseur y est délicate» (p. 53).

national doctrine (p. 207) the use of offensive capabilities and techniques as an accepted and regular means of warfare.[5] One immediate consequence of the 2008 national defense White Paper was indeed the creation of ANSSI, a national agency for the security of information systems.[6]

1.1 The Emergence of Cyber-Domain (1972–2000)

With a lack of shared international and legal framework, the boundaries and contents of domestic national cybersecurity strategies are often unknown by their own nation-states. Information warfare has long been considered as an ancillary arm to conventional warfare, and consequently contained within the eminent domain of military programming. Hence, most of the countries that we studied for this monograph are reluctant, in their published doctrines, to encapsulate information warfare within the framework of national cyber-strategies. The European Union Agency of Network and Information Security Agency (ENISA) acknowledged in 2011 the lack of guidelines and framework for the study of national cybersecurity strategies[7] and gathered an online resource library that list all available documents of National Cyber Security Strategies (NCSS) in the European Union and the world.[8] We used ENISA and publicly available sources to understand and compare 35 national cyber-doctrines and national cyber security strategies for this monograph, in order to depict the founding stones of the French national cyber security strategy in its global context.

This monograph is organized in four sections. The first section, its current introduction, addresses the objective and the methodological pitfalls in the study of national cybersecurity and cyberdefense strategies. The second section of this monograph explores the history of hacking and the birth of cybersecurity as a national doctrine component. It details how the art of hacking slowly transformed itself from a militant and joyful underground practice in the early 1970s, to defense-oriented national embodiments, subject to sovereignty and large-scale computational and informational warfare. The third section explores the determinants of a national cyber security strategy, and applies this framework analysis to the French national cyber security strategy. Finally, the fourth section discusses the forthcoming strategic shifts in cybersecurity (use of artificial intelligence,

---

[5]«L'efficacité à tous niveaux des forces de défense et de sécurité dépend et dépendra de plus en plus du bon fonctionnement de leurs systèmes d'information. La planification et l'exécution d'opérations combinées avec des actions cybernétiques tendent en effet à devenir la norme. Avant même que des cibles physiques ne soient détruites, tout système de défense pourra être en effet désorganisé et partiellement aveuglé au travers de frappes silencieuses et ciblées».

[6]https://www.ssi.gouv.fr/en/.

[7]Luiijf et al. (2011).

[8]ENISA—National cyber security strategies resource centre: https://www.enisa.europa.eu/topics/national-cyber-security-strategies/ncss-map?tab=details.

autonomous learning) and their implications for strategizing and crafting national doctrines for cybersecurity and cyberdefense.

The first chapter allows creating a framework as to identify several classes of cyber attacks. In the pioneering years (1971–1993) most cyber attacks were spontaneous, and most of them would not qualify with contemporary standards, to the label of "aggressions". They were mostly "nondirected"; not that early hackers were clueless, but rather because the hack was itself the aim of the game. For example, J. Draper's "blue box" was motivated by both the discovery of the open vulnerability of telephony system (the direct command through a 2600 Hz whistling input) and by the amusement of Draper in subverting, rather playfully, a telephony system. Most of these early hacks and attacks had immediate effects. A hack was conducted spontaneously, for immediate gains, with cunning and joy at heart, without a specific target in mind. It was an age of talented individuals, trying to get symbolic or small gains, belonging to an underground culture. We called these early years the "code breaking years." Most governments in these early years were already involved in heavy and systematic signal intelligence (SIGINT), inherited from the trauma of World War II. The Silicon Valley itself can be interpreted as the outcome of an effort of the United States to prevail in any further SIGINT confrontation in the event of a global war, as put by Steve Blank in his excellent presentation on that matter.[9] Subsequently, most nations after WWII, and throughout the Cold War, developed distinct national security strategies for electronic warfare, elaborated as a means to prevail in conventional and strategic warfare through communication interceptions. Subsequently, most "cybersecurity" operations (the term is here an anachronism) were conducted by nation-states as ancillary covert operations within the lower and less preeminent national security contexts.

Paradoxically, the traction for more targeted and "long reach" cyber attacks did not come from governmental and national initiatives. Most Cold War operations involved individual (or group) targets, within the framework of an East-West psychological warfare. In the early 1990s, the birth of the cyberspace—i.e. the widespread use of the internet and electronic data exchange—accelerated the rate and scale of cyber-attacks in civil societies, from the First National Bank of Chicago computer theft in 1982 to the democratization of Trojans by hackers' groups in the late 1990s, such as the Cult of Dead Cow. Still, most attack campaigns were led by spontaneously organized cybercriminals, some of them displaying a nearly humorous lack of operational security.

Yet, the "hacking" subculture in this second period (1993–1997) got more organized, with a clear split between *hacktivism* (underground enthusiasts espousing the fight for freedom of expression… and coding) and emergent criminal hacking groups, on payroll of the CIA, the FBI (for sting operations), organized

---

[9]See Steve blank, «The secret history of the Silicon Valley», presentation at UC Berkeley Haas School of Business, Nov. 20, 2008 and associated materials at: https://steveblank.com/secret-history/#Secret%20History%20Backstory.

crime, and rarely but surely, nation-states. This second period, which we called the "birth of the cybercrime," is also one of early intrigues between nation-states, but none of these early confrontations would qualify for cyber warfare, and hence, most nations did not possess, or did not develop, a significant and public national cyber warfare or cyber defense national strategy in this period.

The third period, from 1999 to the mid-2000s, raised both levels of *reach* and *preparation*. The rapid globalization of electronic commerce meant more criminal opportunities, which attracted organized crime. Organized crime had been distant with the cyber security revolution: they were early adopters of encryption tools, long before "cyber-space" was coined as a popular name; they had used chat rooms and IRC to disseminate their ciphers and delivery instructions as soon as the early 1990s; yet, the systematic exploitation of computer crimes either did not yield sufficient returns and, more importantly, the technology was perceived as a threat by older generations that perceived them as a means for the emergence of a more agile and younger organized crime. This perspective changed with the rapid rise of Russian cyber-extortion in early 2001. They saw an opportunity for recurring revenues that could compensate the losses generated by the aftermath of the 1997 world financial crisis. This shift announced a truly systematic and global monetization of cyber-theft.

1.2 The Rise of Cognitive Warfare (1997–2001)

On the governmental side, in the same period, China deployed its Titan Rain attack, which came as a surprise for the G7 and five eyes intelligence communities. It signaled that China had much more advanced preparedness that anticipated. They had a *doctrine*, an *organization* and a national militarized cyber-capability. In the West, cyber-operations were mostly conducted by foreign intelligence services (intrusion, communication interceptions) and domestic counterintelligence (same purposes). They were numerous writings, both public and classified, on the potential use of cyber technologies in the conduct of large-scale warfare, notably the early works of Winn Schwartau in 1994 on information warfare. But these early works were of unequal quality. They mixed "FUDs" (Fear Uncertainty and Doubts) pieces, wolf-crying imprecations with more seriously crafted analysis. Information warfare specialists, even when announcing a dramatic shift from information warfare to cognitive warfare[10] were not considered mainstream. Even when the topic got traction, it never made it to central command, despite, for example, the efforts of the US Air Force to promote the issue in the United States.

[10]See Baumard (1994) and also Stein (1996).

John Arquilla and David Ronfeldt were both extremely instrumental throughout this period in promoting the inclusion of networks and netwars into the US martial ecology. They eventually foresaw the forthcoming hybrid shape and convergence between terror, crime, militancy and cyberspace.[11] What was foreseeable at the end of the 1990s was the forthcoming of a new era of warfare, where information ceases to be an *instrument* of conflict, but instead the *vector* itself. Beyond intelligence, knowledge of the battlefield, adversaries and their intent and capabilities, which all have been eternal components of warfare, the novelty resided in the capacity of defeating an enemy by controlling and enacting its cognitive capabilities.

While this promise remained a mere utopia in the early 1990s, the rise of the Internet in 1998, and the flamboyant demonstration by the PLA with the Titan Rain campaign in 2001, made the prophecy tangible. Warfare was no longer about sheer military dominance and dissuasion. It encompassed the search for durable supremacy of the cognitive apparatus of friends and foes, public opinions, corporate reputations, to the extent of prevailing in conflicts before they would crystallize. Cyberwar was no longer a specialized subdiscipline or contrived arena for special operations. It entered a larger scheme of cognitive supremacy.

We define "cognitive supremacy" as a national core advantage in terms of cognitive capabilities, i.e., the global capability of a nation to detect, process, and make sense of information, stimuli and signals in the military, civil and economic arenas.[12] The main assumption behind this elaboration has been put together in the concept of "improvisational theaters."[13] Increased speed of interventions (simultaneity of forces and large-scale availability of rich and instant media) forced governments and large corporations to operate in real time, through improvised and temporary organizations.

In traditional warfare, a momentum grounded in superior *inertia* and *contingency* of rival forces drives economics of force: the ability to maintain and enforce physical and political presence on a long run leads to the local dominance of a conflict theater. Hypothetically, in information warfare, dominance of electronic and human sources, and information infrastructures, lead to the instantaneous dominance of decision bases. The larger amount of controlled information leads to a large-scale influence of businesses, governmental apparels and eventually, individual decision makers. This doctrine, which emerged in the mid-80s became rapidly obsolete. On one hand, it rapidly appeared that the control of the global information infrastructure would create a strong resistance from individual and businesses. The rather chaotic and swift growth of free contents and alternative access to the Internet led to several confrontations between governments and activists.

---

[11]See: Arquilla and Ronfeldt (2003) and *In Athena's Camp: Preparing for Conflict in the Information Age,* RAND Corporation, 1997. http://www.rand.org/pubs/monograph_reports/MR880.html.

[12]Baumard (2000).

[13]Dearth and Williamson (1996): 25.

On the other hand, dominance of information channels is far to be correlated with a dominance of knowledge generation and the control of information infrastructures.[14] If the gap between information dominance and knowledge advantage was to be widely admitted, the definition and discussion of the new grounds of "cognitive supremacy" had been largely left aside.

Strategic dominance is related to the capability of forbid, enforce or impose a doctrine or a strategic perspective over rivals and allies. Cognitive arenas, i.e., spaces of sensemaking and doctrine construction, are collaborative environments. Engagement and involvement in a world perspective against another one calls for adhesion and belief in the doctrine, the schemata and the value system that underline this perspective. Arquilla suggested that strategic dominance might not be achievable in cyber and perceptual spaces, or even useful.[15]

First, the cyberspace, in the early 2000s, had gained a strong autonomous development. With the democratization of cryptographic tools, and the work of the open source community, most advanced techniques were now freely available. Members and participants of cyber communities had the ability to encrypt, hide, and misrepresent themselves; to use aliases and to decide to withdraw their participation to a community when they felt it was necessary.

Second, the nature of information work allowed every individual to resist any injunction by duplicating or regenerating its dissident voice in any other place of the cyberspace. When Sony tried to stop the proliferation of the DVD cracking software in the late 1990s, more than 200 web sites offering the cracking software appeared on the Internet the following week of the court decision.

Hence, a distinction had to be made between the superiority of the processes and of contents. It is candidly assumed that superior information processes lead to superior information. However, Grinyer and Norburn found a very weak correlation ($r = 0.22$) between the existence of advanced formal planning and firms' profitability.[16] On the contrary, firms with informal strategic planning processes tend to show higher profitability. In other words, a strategic advantage in codified knowledge is not correlated with a higher strategic performance. Before the Norburn and Grinyer' contribution, there was a strong belief that superior knowledge was directly correlated to performance of strategic planning. In terms of national cyber-defense policies, such dominant logic translated into strategies that were mainly focus on gaining a long-term asymmetry in terms of information infrastructures (reach) and offensive capabilities (i.e., outpacing and outscoring opponents).

In fact, most governments and organizations compete with the same information[17] that is to say that the amount and quality of information might not be the core explanation for strategic surprise, success and supremacy. Many large military and

[14]Baumard (1993).

[15]Arquilla (1994).

[16]Grinyer and Norburn (1975).

[17]Starbuck (1992).

economic operations failed despite a huge amount of intelligence: British Airways accumulated a fair amount of accurate intelligence about Virgin Atlantic, and was subsequently condemned for doing so, and yet, did not succeed in preventing Virgin Atlantic to grasp large market share of its London–New York route. Yet, British Airways did not have a cognitive dominance over this particular battlefield: Virgin addressed a new consumer behavior, and did it with innovative marketing tools. The intelligence gathered by BA was formed according to BA's expectations and schemes of what an airline operating between UK and the US should be. The paradox of cognitive warfare, contrary to physical and traditional theaters, is that a heavy and massive attack on a cognitive battlefield can be conducted, without yielding any result.

The terrorist attack on New York's world trade center on September 11, 2001 dramatically changed this perception, resetting idiosyncratic and asymmetric campaigning at the center stage of strategic policymaking. Cyber attacks are, in essence, asymmetric campaigns. They involve the use of cunning intelligence (*hacking*) in defeating a larger and stronger system by detecting its critical flaws, and exploiting them through asymmetric thinking. The main determinants of a successful cyber attack are *speed* and *accuracy*.

Speed is critical as attackers are trying to avoid detection. Avoiding detection is more a matter of time than a matter of the sophistication of decoy. In fact, most efficient deterrence strategies involve delaying the attackers, not defeating them; notably through the use of work factor analysis (WFA).[18] Because attackers are able to transform their offensive vectors in real time (i.e., code morphing), it is very unlikely that signature detection would be timely enough to prevent adversary's intrusion. Adversary work factor analysis allows injecting time bottlenecks in the defense line, which could give a critical advantage to the defender in identifying the attacker, its point of entry or in relating the indicators of compromise with an actual source of attack. Asymmetric campaigning is both a combination of *speed* and *idiosyncrasy*. The attacker needs to defeat the defender's detection model by making sure that his or her code escapes any existing analytical model. This is achieved by obfuscation and by the uniqueness of the attack campaign. But in most cases, speed is an adequate substitute for idiosyncrasy.

Accuracy is the key determinant of the success of an asymmetric campaign, and accordingly, to every successful cyber attack. The less accurate a reconnaissance operation, the more it will leave traces and footprints of its exploration. The only problem is that accuracy takes time. Dahl suggested that this tension between speed and accuracy might be the central element of cognitive dominance.[19] He notes: "The requirement for speed in a dynamic environment tends to call for an intuitive decision process. Conversely, the need for accuracy calls for a more analytical approach. The intuitive process is fast but can lead to poor decisions when a commander's intuitive skills do not fit the problem. This is usually due to

---

[18]See Schudel and Wood (2000) and Van Leeuwen et al. (2015).

[19]Dahl (1996).

insufficient pattern recognition. On the other hand, the analytical approach generally yields accurate decisions but normally takes more time than may be available."[20]

1.3 Early Doctrines of Cognitive Dominance (2001–2005)

In the early 2000s, the assumption that the control over information flows leads toward a cognitive supremacy became heavily challenged. The 1999 US doctrine (from Joint Publication 3-13) unfolded as follows: "Information Operations (IO) capitalize on the growing sophistication, connectivity, and reliance on information technology. IO targets information technology or information systems in order to affect the information-based process whether human or automated. Such information dependent processes range from National Command Authorities-level decision-making to the automated control of key commercial infrastructure such as telecommunications and electric power."[21]

To focus cognitive warfare on information infrastructures was misleading for several reasons: First, information infrastructures benefit from open architectures. A privatization and balkanization of control and ownership would lead to strategic isolation. Moreover, a central command and control that would remotely disable communication systems from a rival country, government or enterprise is improbable given the redundancy and ubiquity of most information infrastructures. Second, the use of brutal force (i.e., disconnecting an opponent's infrastructure) would be detrimental to the world trade as economic retaliation would be highly probable; in other words, the situation in this new era of information warfare is very similar to nuclear dissuasion. Large destructive capabilities can be built, but their use is less than probable.

Hence, legal and competitive cognitive dominance was becoming the more current form of cognitive warfare, contrary to the Joint Doctrine for Information Operations' predictions. Legal and competitive cognitive dominance (LCCD) is the competitive use of national cognitive capabilities in legal and fair competitive practices. Covert cognitive dominance (CCD) is on the contrary the use of misleading and deceptive information operations and technologies in order to achieve unfair and illegal cognitive dominance. CCD encompasses all well-known techniques and practices of decoy, deception and covert influence. The Table 1.1 (below) compares the practices and strategies used in LCCD and CCD: cognitive dominance by numbers, through sensemaking, persuasive and disruptive cognitive dominance and the exploitation of cognitive rents (see Table 1.1).

Table 1.1 opposes two generations of cyber warfare. Inherited from the Cold War, covert cyber operations pursued the proliferation of doctrinal components

---

[20]Ibid., p. 128.

[21]The original text is available on the Internet Archive at: https://archive.org/stream/Misc-DoD/Joint%20Pub%203-13-Joint%20Doctrine%20for%20Information%20Operations_djvu.txt.

Table 1.1 Sensemaking versus infrastructural dominance

	Competitive dominance	Covert dominance
By numbers	*Information infrastructure ownership*: Rivals seek to dominate the development and the contents of GII through commercial and technological offers	*Proliferation*: Doctrines and schemas are intensively proliferated over the cognitive framework (cyber-space, decision infrastructures, publications, large media)
Through sensemaking	*Expertise and learning*: A strategic focus is put on the development of national sensemaking capabilities through education, training programs	*Brain Drain*: Expertise and knowledge intensive firms get large incentives to settle on controlled territories or to behave cooperatively

over the global cognitive infrastructure; which was the emerging Internet in the late 1990s, and would become inclusive of artificial intelligence, deep learning and distributed decision-making after 2010. The Cold War battle for the "hearts and minds" translated into a more distributed confrontation for gaining advantage in the arena of individual decision-making, consumer choices, and mass opinion. However, in such a battlefield, the main vector is the *social network*, which swiftly left governments lagging behind. Another example of covert dominance were brain drain operations, which made sense in the Cold War era, but were quickly losing traction when intellectual capital, ideas, creative commons started to circulate freely in the early 2000s.

The early cyber-warfare doctrines were homothetic to Cold War doctrines. Keywords of early national cyber-defense national strategies were *persuasion, preemption, deterrence and disruption*. Table 1.2, displays examples[22] of what was foreseen as key elements of cognitive warfare in 2000. With distance, they reveal a critical discrepancy in a dominant logic that foresaw a direct transposition from legacy strategic constituents to the Internet era. Persuasion was perceived as top–down process, from a central command toward a population at large. Most Internet service providers were still struggling in the late 1990s whether to consider the Internet as a "digital media", providing "channels", "portals", "walled gardens", which were very similar in design and philosophy with traditional broadcasting. Facebook was displaying a static page (the "wall") as if a screen could not be anything else than a fixed window on the world. Both governments and early champions of the net economy were seeking "cognitive rents", i.e., accumulating sources, encouraging knowledge retention and capitalization. Accordingly, early cyber-war doctrines were narrowly focused on restricting knowledge flows and restraining knowledge mobility.

Transpositions of military models to the new competition led policymakers and intelligence agencies to strongly believe that the new capabilities of the information

[22]Table extract from Baumard (2000).

Table 1.2 Legacy paradigms of cognitive dominance in the late 1990s

	Competitive cognitive dominance	Covert cognitive dominance
Persuasive	*Lobbying and soft influence*: Representatives at large defend the organization's perspective (consultants, lawyers, opinion leaders) *Netwars*: Use of social networks and the Internet to globally influence opinion	*Deception and PsyOps*: Psychological operations and information operations are aimed to dissimulate reality, or to simulate favorable schemas and doctrines
Cognitive rents	*Intellectual capital and knowledge generation*: Incentives are developed in order to encourage knowledge retention and capitalization	*Knowledge preemption*: New knowledge and discoveries are taken over in offensive educative LBOs. Rules and regulations restrain knowledge mobility
Disruptive	*Disruption of the speed and consistency of rivals' decision cycles*: Deliberate ambiguities are designed to paralyze the decision cycle of rivals	*Deception*: Deceptive knowledge is implemented in rivals' decision processes and mental models in order to unethically paralyze and mislead rivals' decision-making and knowledge generation

infrastructure should be exploited in implementing a new breadth of covert manipulation of information and knowledge. This early perception (1997–2005) was misleading in several aspects. The main characteristic of the new global information infrastructure was to offer more degrees of freedom to individual expression. This brought more spontaneity to knowledge exchange and knowledge generation than ever reached in precedent eras. Spontaneous knowledge exchange favored immediate sensemaking over accumulation and hierarchical cycles of knowledge exploitation. Spontaneous knowledge exchange required interpersonal trust, while bureaucratic knowledge control required institutional control. Institutions started to compete with unpredictable swarm of spontaneous public opinions, progressively losing most of their strongholds.

Most nations involved in offensive cyber-campaigning in the early 2000s simply ignored this shift. Most doctrines did not encompass the influence of openness and basic principles of freedom of expression. The Russian Information Security Doctrine, approved on September 9, 2000, represents an example of one of those early doctrines that simply duplicated a Cold War agenda into a global digital world.[23] It enforced a principle of inseparability between public information, including the Russian Press, the mass media and the Internet.[24] The first section of

[23]For a thorough analysis, see Deppe (2005).

[24]This principal of inseparability between public information, the Russian people and the State would become the main obstacle for the cooperation of Russia within the international legal framework of the Budapest Convention, a year later, in 2001. The Treaty was never ratified by Russia.

the Russian information security doctrine of 2000 depicts the digitalization of society as follows: "The present stage in the development of society is characterized by the growing role of the information sphere which represents a combination of information, the information infrastructure, the agents that gather, form, disseminate and use information as well as the system of regulating the social relations arising from this. The information sphere, being a pivotal element in the life of society, exerts a strong influence on the state of the political, economic, defense and other components of the security of the Russian Federation."[25] Most of this doctrine prevailed until its replacement[26] in December 2016. It enforced a vertically controlled vision of cyber-sovereignty that would prevail in Russia for the next 16 years (2000–2016).

1.4 The Birth of National Cybersecurity Strategies (2006–2016)

In early 2006, US SIGINT obtained confirmation that the Chinese People Liberation Army (PLA) was concentrating an unprecedented number of military cybersecurity personnel Datong Road in Gaoqiazohen in Shanghai's Pudong district.[27] The unit 61,398 was estimated to have enrolled hundreds of military signal, electronic warfare and hacking experts, and was, according to Fireye, provided with a dedicated fiber optic communication infrastructure. Mandiant, which was later acquired by Fireye, identified Unit 61,398 as a key coordinator in the launch of a worldwide advanced persistent threat (APT) campaign that they named APT1.

APT1, according to Mandiant, which gathered evidence and indicators of compromise and made it available to the public in the same report, had compromised 141 large corporations in 20 industries worldwide, spanning from defense, nuclear, energy, telecommunications, etc. APT1 was not a sophisticated campaign. It used well-known exploits, most of them being simple phishing techniques of injecting code in the targeted systems by asking e-mail recipients to open an

[25]Russian Information Security Doctrine, Sept. 9, 2000. Translation and quote from K.M. Deppe, op.cit., p. 26.

[26]The new Information Security Doctrine of Russia was enacted on December 5, 2016, revoking the Sept 9, 2000 Pr—1895 framework. It enlarges the initial concept of information security to include: "n this doctrine under the information sphere is understood collection of information, facilities information, information systems and websites in the information and telecommunication network "Internet" (Hereinafter—the "Internet" network), communications networks, information technology, entities, which activity is connected with the formation and information processing, development and use of these technology, information security, as well as the totality of the relevant public regulation mechanisms relationship."

[27]This information was breached in Fireye's report on APT1, and denied by Chinese authorities. https://www.fireeye.com/content/dam/fireeye-www/services/pdfs/mandiant-apt1-report.pdf.

attachment (and most commonly a PDF file). Mandiant estimated that APT1 subsequently compromised hundreds of thousands points of access, with an average stay of 356 days, with the longest compromission being 1764 days, and the largest data theft reaching 6.5 terabytes for a single organization.[28] One of the recurrent targets, according to the same report, were the US Department of Homeland Security's servers.

APT1 was considered as a strong evidence for many countries that cognitive warfare had left the realm of theoretical fantasies. The Mandiant's report was designed as to propagate this idea. Uncommon to the art, the Mandiant report was disclosing the real names and addresses (by displaying their Military Identity cards) of the alleged Chinese military hackers. A traditional incident report would disclose evidence of a hacking activity (by disclosing the hashes of malware and indicators of compromise), and eventually the pseudonyms or the known trademark of hackers' groups. But Mandiant's report was different. It disclosed the pseudonyms of the hackers being part of the operation ("Ugly Gorilla", "Dota", "SuperHard", etc.), and then proceeded to disclose their supposed real names. Mandiant also disclosed 3000 APT1 indicators, such as domain names, IP addresses and MD5 hashes of malware, including a sample of Indicators of compromise (IOCs).

The defacing campaign on Estonia was second event that changed the mindset of national cybersecurity strategies in April 2007. The attacks consisted of a traditional distributed denial of service (DDOS) campaigns, borrowing bandwidth from privately owned servers. In a second phase, many governmental websites were defaced.[29] The overall campaign lasted 22 days until May 18, 2007. This attack, although not spectacular, was targeting a large arrays of governmental servers, and was targeting an overall national infrastructure, even if the whole population of Estonia, around 1,320,000 habitants, is smaller than most Chinese cities. But Estonia was a highly symbolic target as it had developed close relationships with the United States in the precise domain of national cybersecurity strategies and deterrence. Most analysts perceived the campaign as a warning from Russia, informing the United States that its cyber-proselytism was getting too close to its national borders. On one hand, the deterrence and contingency response deployed by Estonian's incident response teams were timely, and the attack did not create any extensive damage. On the other hand, the Estonian government was incapable of attributing the attacks to a precise Russian organization. They came up with highly debatable indicators of compromise, which were pointing to an IP address directly located inside the Kremlin (undoubtedly improbable), and other IOCs indicating the

---

[28]Mandiant/Fireye' APT1 report, op. cit., p. 3. According to the report: "In 1849 of the 1905 (97%) of the Remote Desktop sessions APT1 conducted under our observation, the APT1 operator's keyboard layout setting was "Chinese (Simplified)—US Keyboard". Microsoft's Remote Desktop client configures this setting automatically based on the selected language on the client system. Therefore, the APT1 attackers likely have their Microsoft operating system configured to display Simplified Chinese fonts. 817 of the 832 (98%) IP addresses logging into APT1 controlled systems using Remote Desktop resolved back to China" ibid., p. 24.

[29]Goodman (2010).

involvement of an independent Russian hacking criminal organization. At the end, Estonian government officials had to admit that they had been unable to attribute the attacks to Russia, even they were intimately convinced it was the case.

The Chinese and the Russian–Estonian cases triggered a wake-up call in most nations. In both cases, there was no absolute attribution of the attacks. In the APT1 case, 98% of attacks could be related to Chinese IP addresses but it does not mean that these IP addresses belonged to governmental organizations. Most of the hacking tools used in APT1 were widely available, which meant that even if China had been directly involved, the case would not hold in an international legal court. In the Estonian case, the evidence was shallower. Most experts were dumbfounded by initial attributions tracing the point of origin of the attack in a Putin's department. The two cases demonstrated than any foreign power could rather freely, and without any accountability, engaged in a large-scale destabilization campaign of civil infrastructures. The cases also demonstrated the poor cyber resilience of both military and civil infrastructures in the potential deterrence of a large-scale attack. Cyber warfare's new dominant logic was very different from what had been expected and drafted during the "cognitive warfare" doctrinal era (2001–2006).

This book addresses the French national strategy for cyber-security within this historical perspective. It does address neither any organizational charts, nor a cumbersome list of rules and regulations of cybersecurity in France. The objective is, in a first section, to understand the technological and social evolution of cyber attacks, from the genuinely enthusiastic hacking from the early 1970s to the more brutal and criminalized cyber-thefts and State-sponsored aggressions that emerged in the 2006–2016 period.

From this historical perspective, in a second chapter, we will investigate the determinants of a national strategy for cyber-defense. In this second chapter, we will pay a particular attention to the difficulties of designing adequate and legitimate countermeasures, in the face of unrealizable attributions, morphing attack codes, and artificial intelligence-assisted attack campaigns. We will eventually understand why we are still lacking a shared international legal framework for cooperation in cyber-conflict resolution. This second chapter ends with a timeline of the evolution of the French national strategy for cybersecurity and cyber-defense.

The fourth and last chapter of this book compares the cybersecurity national doctrines that resulted from the evolution of *attack vectors*, announcing the emergence of a "behavioral intelligence paradigm," both in attack and defense. Based on the analysis of publicly available documents from 35 countries, we map and position each national cybersecurity strategy on a 2×2 matrix, offering a classification of national cybersecurity doctrines in four categories: "societal resilience", "power-sovereign", "social order" and "technocratic". On this matrix, France displays a clear shift between its "*Livre blanc*" *de la Défense* (national white paper, 2008) and its latest cyber-defense and cybersecurity national strategies, respectively enacted in 2015 and 2016. Finally, the book offers a review of forthcoming critical technological shifts in the field of detection of cyber-threats. Namely, the last section of this book explores the rise of artificial intelligence both in the field of advanced persistent threats (APTs) and in new deterrence strategies.

References

Arquilla J (1994) The strategic implications of strategic dominance. Strateg Rev 22(3):24–30

Arquilla J, Ronfeldt D (2003) Networks and netwars: The Future of Terror, Crime and Militancy, RAND Corporation

Baumard Ph (1993) From noticing to making sense: using intelligence to develop strategy. Int J Intel Counterintelligence 7(1):29–73

Baumard Ph (1994) From information warfare to knowledge warfare: preparing for the paradigm shift. In: Schwartau W (ed) Information warfare. Thunder's Mouth Press, New York, pp 611–626

Baumard Ph (2000) From inertia warfare to cognitive warfare: economics of force in cognitive arenas. Martial ecologies: towards a new strategic discourse, Tel Aviv, May 30, conference proceedings, organized by Tel Aviv University and the Jaffee Center for Strategic Studies

Dahl AB (1996) Command dysfunction: minding the cognitive war, a thesis presented to the faculty of the school of advanced airpower studies. Maxwell Air force Base, Alabama

Dearth DH, Williamson CA (1996) Information age, information war: where are we in history? In: Campen AD, Dearth DH, Goodden RT (eds) Cyberwar: security, strategy and conflict in the information age, fairfax. AFCEA, VA

Deppe KM (2005) The media and democracy in Russia, Ph Dissertation, Naval Postgraduate School, Monterey, CA, June, pp 25–30

Goodman W (2010) Cyber deterrence: tougher in theory than in practice? Strateg Stud Q Fall pp 102–135

Grinyer PH, Norburn D (1975) Planning for existing markets: perceptions of executives and financial performance. J R Stat Soc Ser A 138:336–372

Luiijf H, Besseling K, Spoelstra M, de Graaf P (2011) Ten national cyber security strategies: a comparison. In: CRITIS 2011—6th international conference on critical information infrastructures security

Schudel G, Wood B (2000) Adversary work factor as a metric of information assurance. Proceedings of the workshop on new security paradigms pp 23–30

Starbuck WH (1992) Strategizing in the real world. Int J Technol manag Spec Publ Technol Found Strateg Manage 8(1/2)

Stein G (1996) US Information Warfare. Jane's Information Group, NY

Van Leeuwen B, Stout WMS, Urias V (2015) Operational cost of deploying moving target defenses defensive work factors. Military communications conference, MILCOM IEEE

Chapter 2
A Brief History of Hacking and Cyberdefense

Abstract This chapter investigates the technological evolution of cyber-crimes from its emergence in the early 1980s to its latest developments in 2013. From this evolution, we draw implications for doctrines, policy, innovation incentives, and roadmaps as we propose the emergence of a new "behavioral intelligence" paradigm, both in the attack and defense arenas.

Keywords Hacking · Hackers · History of hackers · Ethical hacking · White hacking · Cracking · Computer heists · Hactivism · Cyber-criminality

2.1 From Defying *Authority* to Defying *Sovereignty*

"Hacking" is defined as the art of finding an astute and elegant solution to an uncommon or undocumented problem, "for enjoyment", as noted by the 2016 edition of the Merriam-Webster dictionary. Most contemporary dictionaries are struggling to find a correct definition of hacking. Half of them would oppose "hacking" with "cracking" as if an invisible moral line would be a sufficient etymology guideline to entrust a solid definition. It is indeed a fallacy, as "crackers" never defined themselves as adversaries of hackers! As a teenager in the late 1970s, I would try to "crack" passwords or machine code to copy a game and change few lines of its code. "Hacking" was a already a verb that signified "cutting through a dense forest" since the middle age; and "cutting through a difficult technical obstacle" since the Tech Model Railroad Club of MIT in April, 1955, requested "that anyone working or hacking on the electrical system turn the power off to avoid fuse blowing."[1]

[1]«A short history of hack», Ben Yagod, *The New Yorker, March* 6, 2014 http://www.newyorker.com/tech/elements/a-short-history-of-hack.

P. Baumard, *Cybersecurity in France*, SpringerBriefs in Cybersecurity,
DOI 10.1007/978-3-319-54308-6_2

This definition lasted against any other attempts to turn "hacking" into a dark and illegal realm: functional medicine professionals propose to "hack" your diet; health gurus suggest they found a "life hacking" technique to make your daily routine better. Albeit, here again, this could well be an ugly deformation of the verb "to hack", which is, by essence, devoid of peculiar or monetary interests.

A true hacker, in mind and spirit, is seeking the "hack value"[2] as a self-sufficient motivation to enthusiastically pursue the de-routing of *any system*. Hacking is a joyful exploration of the hidden and unsuspected capabilities, or flaws, of any technical system in order to stretch them into novel function, through their intimate understanding, breaking, and reconstruction. Hacking is before all an *intellectual challenge* that can be joyfully owned and discovered by the most pragmatic and anti-intellectual individuals. Hence, a hacker shall not display any elitist behaviors, even if the only mean of recognition and mutual appreciation is, indeed, the demonstration of unique skills.

The hacking subculture might well be so enduring because of its numerous ambiguous anchors. Pioneer hacker Eric S. Raymond has been struggling for 15 years (2001–2017) to put together an online guideline entitled "*How to become a hacker*".[3] The more he tried to codify a "rule book" of hacker's behavior, values, and determinants, the less it persuaded the ever-evolving hacking community: to the point of most younger hackers today, a.k.a. 2017, ignore who E.S. Raymond is.

Eric Raymond, however, has captured essential traits of the hacker culture: it is a "mindset not confined to the software-hacker culture"; it is an attitude that involves solving problems and harmlessly doing so, even if the consequence of this problem-solving implies unveiling a vulnerability in a critical system; it involves defending the fundamental freedom of expression, and doing so competently.

"Cyber-crime" refers to the unlawful use of digital, electronic, and software capabilities to misuse, temper, devoid, destruct, or influence public or private information systems. Cybernetic and informational components may not be the primary target or final outcomes of cyber-crime campaigns.

Hence, "hacking" and "cyber-crime" have nothing in common; even if they use programming and coding skills as a common language; but everyone uses a computer, and using a computer does not make everyone a dangerous cybercriminal. Hacking is joyful culture of excellence, which is at the center of most essential scientific discoveries of the twentieth and twenty-first centuries. A good scientist is a hacker as he or she never rests satisfied with a partial answer to a research question; will always seek to find an astute and unsuspected research design to solve a resistant obstacle; will do so with humility; and will seek scientific competition for the advancement of knowledge, and not the advancement of his or her ego.

[2]http://www.catb.org/~esr/jargon/html/H/hack-value.html.

[3]http://www.catb.org/~esr/faqs/hacker-howto.html.

2.2 Exploration Years

The term "hacking" escaped its nurturing and birthplace ground at MIT in the mid-1960s. It did so with the ingenious hacking of telephony systems by the use of the then-open 2600 Hz frequency. The conversation started in the MIT student newspaper reported that telephone services "have been curtailed because of so-called 'hackers'"; the hackers having "accomplished such things as tying up all the tie-lines between Harvard and M.I.T., or making long-distance calls by charging them to a local radar installation"[4] in 1963. By leaving the MIT lab playgrounds, it entered a more societal sandbox, which immediately captured the malicious meddling potential of the game, and came up with the "black hat" hacking denomination. The concept of conducting a crime by computer became popular in the 1970s, culminating in 1976 with the publication of Donn B. Parker's book, *Crime by computer*, which ending would appear today as the most inaccurate description of the craft.[5]

The origin of cyber-crime per se is concomitant with the pioneering efforts of technology enthusiasts in exploring the possibilities offered by technological innovation. Exploration and autonomous appropriation are still, to date, a core motivation in the creation of "hacks". John Draper was one of these computer enthusiasts who helped popularize the first "phreaking" hack, consisting of a multi-frequency tone generator, late known as the Blue Box to pitch the exact 2600 Hz frequency to hack into the long-distance phone system of AT&T in the early 1970s.

Most of early attacks were *spontaneous*, motivated by technology exploration, non-directed (without a specific target in mind) and immediate in their effects.[6] With the rise of personal computers, these early pioneers of hacking started to group in spontaneous associations, espousing discourses of the times on individual freedom, resistance to authority, amusement with detours of emerging technologies. Phreaking and hacking became both shared practices that cemented long friendships between developers, industry pioneers (Wozniak, Jobs, etc.), and politically motivated technology enthusiasts. The borders between an emerging underground culture (yippee, hackers) and a criminal subculture were blurry and unstable, with very little self-regulation, and comprising teenagers, advanced computer developers, and self-taught technology explorers.[7] We call this era the "code breaking years", where talented individuals are mostly motivated by symbolic and small gains, a feeling of belonging to a new community and self-identity.

France had a very dynamic community of these young hackers as early as the late 1970s. France pioneered many of the telecommunication industry's radical innovations, in large part thanks to its public laboratories: CNRS (national scientific

---

[4]Ben Yagoda, op. cit., 2014.

[5]http://www.nytimes.com/1976/06/13/archives/crime-by-computer.html?_r=0.

[6]Cf. Raymond (2000).

[7]Katie and Markoff (1995).

research center) and INRIA (the national institute for computer research and automation, created in 1967). The ancestor of the Internet, the "Cyclades Network" was an Inria's creation in 1971. After a visit of Bolt, Beranek and Newman (BBN) in 1970 by the director of INRIA, several emerging languages and systems were introduced in France: the Logo language and the Tenex exploitation system. At the time, all the French administrations wanted to set up their own databases. The universities were cooperating on the project through research contracts and the general delegation to computing, led by Maurice Allègre, wanted to interconnect them via a data network. Louis Pouzin brought together a small team of six people, which started in 1971, and chose people outside of INRIA as Jean-Louis Grange, Jean-Pierre Touchard, Michel Elie, Jean Le Bihan, and Gérard Le Lann, to conduct a studying mission within Arpanet in 1973.

In the spring of 1972, Louis Pouzin, on tour in the United States, noted some "insufficiently practical aspects of Arpanet," which led Cyclade to introduce additional functions and simplify others. "Pouzin's work has brought us a lot," says Vinton Cerf, "We used its flow control system for the TCP/IP protocol. It was motivating to talk to him."[8] Cyclades, unfortunately, was abandoned shortly after its birth, around 1976.

The combination of strong curricula in mathematics and applied university education in computer programming led France to develop a unique academic culture in computer science as early as the mid-1960s. Jacques Arsac developed Exel in 1973 (for algorithmic description). In 1972, Alain Colmerauer and Philippe Roussel created the programming language Prolog. The same year, François Gernelle developed the first microcomputer at INRA, based on the Intel 8008 microprocessor. The Micral N was introduced to the market in April 1973, which will later be integrated by Bull Microsystems as the "Bull Micral". The number of French computer science pioneers in the domain of algorithmic, artificial intelligence, programming languages, software architecture, and applied mathematics for computer science is outstanding: Henri Gouraud, Philippe Flajolet, Henri Gouraud, Gérard Huet, Gilles Kahn, Bertrand Meyer, Jean Ichbiah (Ada language), Roland Moreno, Jacques Pitrat, Jean Dominique Warnier ("the Warnier/Orr diagram"), etc.

The outcome of this pioneering year is a subculture of hacking deeply rooted in mathematical groundings: formulation, programming languages, mathematical proofing, etc. Compared to other European hacking communities, especially German, English, or American, the French initial "hacking" community is an offspring of elitist engineering schools. These early adopters contributed to the creation of a peculiar French computer science's culture, based on experimental investigations, creative coding, and never too far from its mathematical roots. In the early 1980s, when computer sciences became a mainstream educational offer, the French computer sciences and hacking community were already part of the most intellectually advanced groups in Europe.

[8]«Et la France ne créa pas l'Internet», par Laurent Mauriac et Emmanuelle Peyret, dans *Libération* du 27 mars 1998.

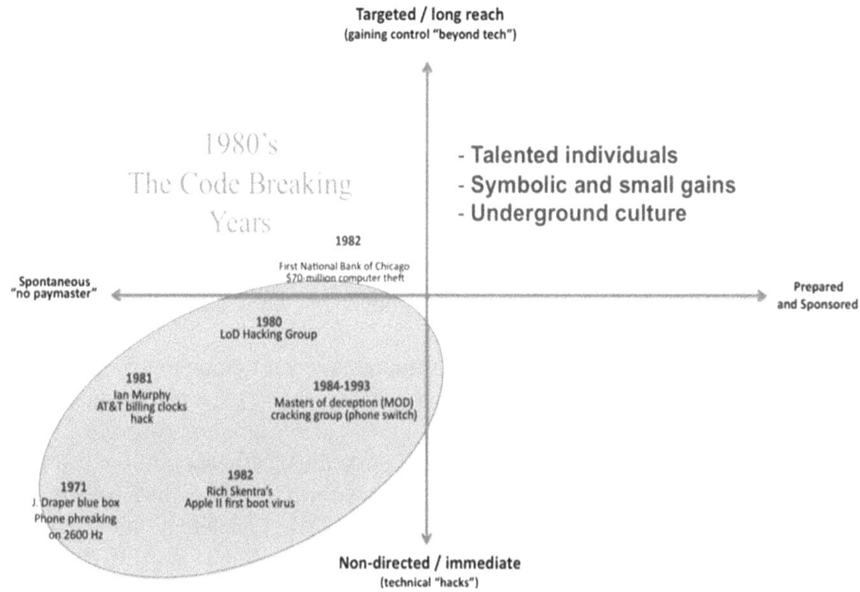

Fig. 2.1 The early years: the code-breaking paradigm

In the mid-1980s, technical bulletin boards from hackers' groups started to disclose attack guidelines for intrusions, sometimes both physical and code-based (such as the first issue of the Legion of Doom LOD/H Technical Journal, on Jan. 1, 1987[9]). LOD and MOD (Masters of Deception), hence, became influential in transforming these early movements into more organized "cracking" communities, moving a step away from the original hacking culture (see Fig. 2.1). MOD initiated a real hacking group culture in the 1980s by instituting degrees of initiation (and skills) as a filter for knowledge access. The group was acknowledged for its introduction of a non-formalized code of ethics, that implied that knowledge that could be harmful to the public shall not been released irresponsibly. LOD used a similar compartmentalization of hacking knowledge in the early 1980s. The FBI unfortunately, hastily dismantled most of these pioneering hacking groups in the early 1990s. Five founding members of MOD were indicted in 1992 in Federal Court.

The archetypal hacking group of the early 1980s is of course the Chaos Computer Club (CCC), formed in Berlin on September 2, 1981. Contrary to its predecessors, the CCC adopted a clear political agenda with a strong commitment to the defense of all forms of freedom: freedom of expression, human rights, and political self-determination. The refusal of any form of "paymaster" in any of its

[9]http://www.textfiles.com/magazines/LOD/lod-1.

political struggles, technical demonstrations, and the pursuit of a flamboyant and artistic communication literally created the founding stones of the hacker culture.

Every hack had a demonstrative purpose, in defense of the general public. For instance, they hacked into the German *Bildschirmtext* service (a pioneering European service for text messaging), attributing DM 134,000 to the CCC, that they returned the next day. Their implication in the fight for the reunification of Germany, while still disputed today, is known to have been decisive in specific cases. The group was successful in maintaining its founding culture throughout the 1980s and the 1990s; demonstrating flows in Microsoft ActiveX technology in 1996; cloning GSM cards in 1998 (by breaking the COMP128 encryption algorithm).

The "Hacking Group" subculture never found any solid grounding in France in the early 1980s and 1990s. This can be in part explained by the large availability of public computer systems, mainframes in French universities during the 1980s. France was a strategic partner of IBM, which pushed the early adoption of "Bitnet" in France as soon as 1984. French computer science students had a free and common access to computation and software, maybe impeding the need for building independent resources. Most French hackers of the early 1990s were isolated, or acting within small groups of friends from the same engineering schools. Before 1993, without any Internet service provider, the French hacking community was dependent on university resources, and more or less-reliable self-deployed telecommunication solutions.[10]

With the launch of WorldNet in 1993, a few spontaneous, and self-proclaimed, French "hacking groups" emerged. Despite various vigorous claims of self-proclaimed "French hacking pioneers", there were not many steady and regular hacking groups in France in between the late 1980s up to the mid-1990s. There were several passionate individuals who discussed the "telematic revolution" on electronic bulletin boards, some of them turning later into astute and growth-hungry businessmen. In the mid-1990s, a few e-zine such as NoRoute were presumably available, according to N. Ankara (ibid.). As a witness and participant to the scene from 1984 to 1994, my direct observations indicate an underground hacking arena made of friendships, interpersonal collaborations, mostly inspired by the American and German hacking groups, and yielding very sparse organized hacking groups.[11] A lot of urban legends spontaneously spawned in France in the mid-1990s. For instance, the first Linux worm, "ADM",[12] which would basically send a crafted packet on port 53 as to trigger was on the first buffer overflow attack in a Bind DNS

[10]Ankara (2007).

[11]I started the SIM (strategic information management) list and bulletin boards on «Bitnet», the IBM sponsored facsimile and ancestor of the Internet in 1985. Although the group reached more than 500 members very early on, most discussions and sources were drained by US examples. For more details see: Baumard (1991). The first chapter of the book contains a synthesis of the SIM-List experiment.

[12]http://virus.wikidot.com/adm.

server (and then run root privileges) was quickly nicknamed "Association De Malfaiteurs" by early French hacker-apprentices, but "Adm creates the user account w0rm with no password and a suid shell with root privileges in the/tmp directory named .w0rm on the target machine",[13] which did not indicate ownership and was designed so. Even if the worm is attributed to the "Adm Crew", which is supposed to be a German group (who famously hacked the Defcon webpage in 1999 inserting a joke about the US president attending the convention).

An active hacking pioneer in the late 1990s was Vincent Plousey, a.k.a. "Larsen" who was running a small website publishing known, and less known, radiofrequencies under the "Chaos Radio Club of France".[14] Plousey was a municipal telephony network employee who developed a personal passion for everything related to hacking and secret communication. He was arrested on April 18, 2000, for disseminating the frequencies of the French intelligence service (DST), but most of Larsen's diffusions were just copy and paste from American journals, such as the *Monitoring Times* or *Popular Communications*. If he did disseminate the French intelligence service radio coordinates, they were well known by every radio amateur of the times. He finally spent 59 nights in jail in La Santé in Paris. He later admitted that although he joined the early amateur French hacking group "NoRoute", Larsen did not possess sufficient technical knowledge to conduct real network intrusion or password cracking.[15]

Other young hackers from the mid-1990s, such as MJ13, published simple Windows exploits online, and eventually, more colloquial physical hacks (such as piercing the electricity supply counter with a burning red pin).[16] Most of the early French hacking community could be found as editors and contributors of the early pHRACK online magazines, such as Gaius (identified by his acz@vaubansys.com) or kil3r (identified by his kil3r@hert.org).[17] According to Ankara (op. cit.), Gaius was "renown for his social engineering hacks into FBI and CIA telephone network. Surprisingly, he never got jailed but at some point he had to move from the country, officially to escape authorities. HERT was never a hacking group but included a lot of hackers from other international groups such as ADM, w00w00, TESO, and others."

The Cold War and the underground battle for a free Berlin played a determinant role in the evolution of the hacking culture of the late 1980s. The Clifford Stoll episode (a LBL astronomer who accidentally discovered a computer intrusion from West Germany in his laboratory) was the first case to raise the importance of agency coordination and the difficulties of attribution in international computer attacks (Stoll 1989). This case is also one of the early symptoms (1986) of yet to come

---

[13]See «behavior», in http://virus.wikidot.com/adm.

[14]http://n8on.free.fr/hackzines/hvu/8/HVU8.html.

[15]http://probe.20minutes-blogs.fr/tag/bidouille.

[16]A «MJ13» hack page example: http://loginz.chez.com/mj13v2.htm or alternatively: http://n8on.free.fr/hackzines/mj13/.

[17]http://www.digitalsec.net/stuff/website-mirrors/pHC/60/p60-0x01.txt.

advanced persistent threats, highlighting the complexity and sophistication of intrusion campaigns (for details see Stoll's article, 1988[18]).

The early 1990s are hence concomitant with the emergence of criminal subculture of hacking. In the 1980s, cracking events that led to theft or large-scale attacks were rare. Two notable exceptions are the 1986 Pak Brain logic bomb, known as the first virus, and the 1982 First National Bank of Chicago computer theft ($70 M USD). The "Great Hacker War" (conflict between Masters of Deception and Legion of Doom, circa 1991–1992) is an example—today disputed as an exaggeration of trivial confrontations—of the interpersonal dynamics of the early 1990s. A blend of prestige seeking, bravados, and playfulness were the core incentives of these early confrontations.[19] The publication of exploits by hackers' groups triggered, however, the interest of Law enforcement. Operation Sundevil, in 1990, was hence the first large-scale cyber-enforcement operation, involving 15 US cities and leading to three arrests.[20] Most cyber-crimes involved wire-tapping, calling card fraud, and credit card fraud. The relative failure of this operation led to an increase awareness of the central role of cyber-deterrence for federal agencies (Sterling 1994).

Publications such as 2600 and the rise of the cyber-space participated to a democratization of cracking, phreaking, and hacking techniques, which render them more versatile to their use "beyond technology". Focus on distant control, resident threats (democratization of Trojans) creates both a more organized criminal subculture and the birth of a societal reach for attacks (see Fig. 2.2).

France became a very peculiar case in the European hacking communities. Much inspired by the Robert David Steele's experience in creating a "bridge" between the American intelligence community and the hacking community in the early 1990s (by the creation of the open-source community "open-source solutions"[21]), the French domestic intelligence service initiated a similar strategy in 1992. Contrary to Steele's initiative, which was indeed somehow "open", the French DST decided on a large deception campaign, inventing a fake "Chaos Computer Club France". Jean-Bernard Condat[22] launched the fake club in Lyon in 1989, under the orders of DST, as to create a social engineering *honeypot* to uncover and list the names of the emergent hackers in France. The DST sting operation allowed the French intelligence service to identify 2500 active French hackers in the early 1990s.[23] The false flag operation included an online publication, the *Chaos Digest*, which allowed the French intelligence service to gain a tremendous learning experience in early intrusion techniques, as well as engaging into searching and hiring candidates for its

[18]http://pdf.textfiles.com/academics/wilyhacker.pdf.

[19]http://www.textfiles.com/hacking/modbook4.txt.

[20]Clapes (1993).

[21]https://www.theguardian.com/environment/earth-insight/2014/jun/19/open-source-revolution-conquer-one-percent-cia-spy.

[22]Condat's interview: http://www.magic.be/InterieurNuit/SiteMars/Condat.html.

[23]Guisnel (1995).

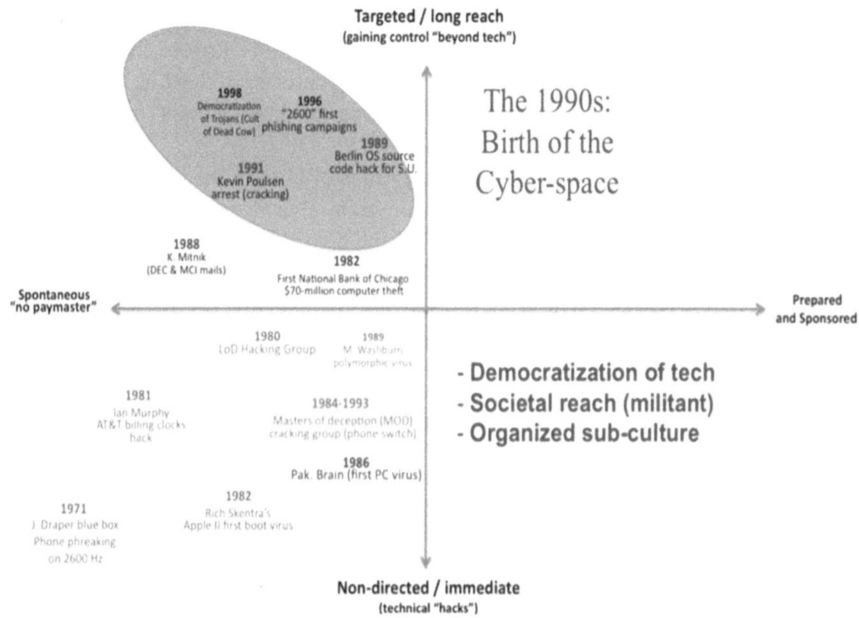

Fig. 2.2 The 1990s: The democratization of cyber-crime

own ranks.[24] Condat later acknowledged that he gave 1030 names of hackers, crackers, and potential cyber-criminals to the French intelligence service. The false flag operation went as far as creating a television prime time show, where the young Jean-Bernard Condat was demonstrating his hacking skills by hacking "live" the bank account of one of the directors of the French intelligence service, the DST.[25]

The very young Condat was wearing a ridiculous white tee shirt with the letters "CCCF" printed on his chest. After this successful DST's false flag operation, as Ankara noted (op. cit.) "most of the old school hackers decided to stop contributing to the scene, which went even more underground, to avoid infiltration of services." The CCCF story had a tremendous and lasting effect on the French hacking community: it has learned more on the French intelligence services than it would ever have. Defiance toward anything governmental started to spread. Most French true hacking groups became surrounded with "op sec" precautions that were not taken by American or German hacking groups. In the early 2000s, the French DST starting to use most of its leads to engage into a large-scale arrest campaign, busting many of the young hackers who dared to make public appearance or online postings. This event also started an internal war between French intelligence services. The military branch, the DGSE, in charge of counter-intelligence and surveillance

[24]Warusfel (2000).

[25]The actual footage of this show is visible on the video archive website of the Institut national audiovisuel: http://www.ina.fr/video/CPB91012010.

of active and nefarious foreign hacking groups, was very upset by the whole amateurism of the "Condat/CCCF" false flag operation. It destroyed the credibility of French intelligence services, and internally, executives of the foreign services harshly complained and tried to stop any kind of involvement of DST into cyber-criminality matters.

The main outcomes of the early sting operations of DST in the mid 1990s were a more alert French underground hacking community, always on the defensive; and a strengthened DGSE offensive hacking arm, as the then Prime Minister clearly heard the arguments of the military branch: DST could not be trusted; a strong offensive unit was going to be built within the better guarded walls of DGSE.

2.3 Hackers Versus Cyber-Criminals: The Monetization's Years

While most attack preparations were targeted on single point of entry in the 1990s, the early 2000s were adopting a whole new perspective. The rise of electronic commerce meant a better monetization of cyber-crime with an expectation of large-scale profits for organized crime. The digitalization of the cultural industry (MP3 s, DVDs) created an appeal for the popular growth of *cracking*. Profiles of hackers accordingly change in two directions: on one hand, amateur crackers (script kiddies, carders) started to use available tools (P2P file sharing, cracking "CDs"). On the other hand, malware production became a profitable black market. Corruption of DNS paths, denial-of-service attacks, defacing campaigns, and corporate thefts found a rapid monetization. The years 2000–2002 were among the most active in malware generation with viruses such as ILOVEYOU, Klez.h., Code Red, etc. The "Iloveyouvirus" spreaded within an email message with its own name as a subject line, and a "love-letter-for-you.txt.vbs" as an attachment. It exploited a flaw from Windows at that time, which would hide, by default, some extensions, including VBS. The malware was a very simple set of instructions in Visual Basic, overwriting random files such as Office files, audio files, and then sent of copy of itself to all people present in the target's address book. The key to the success of ILOVEYOU lied in its simplicity: it used libraries that were already present on all machines (MSFT); its propagation was simple and immediate; it harmed *randomly*, often leaving the victims clueless of what had been erased for a while. Within a month the ILOVEYOU virus made around USD$ 9 billion of damage worldwide.

The group Anonymous was created in 2003 as a loosely coupled and spontaneous coordination of various interests, ranging from militant activism, cracking techniques sharing, and image sharing around the 4chan platform. Massive raids and pranks, known as "4chan raids", popularized a perspective of hacking as a blend of activism, bullying, and satirist information campaigns, although opting out political campaigns in the early years (2003–2006).

In France, many of the early hacking community members went either totally dark (leaving the scene), or persistently underground (publishing less, changing their pseudonyms). Phrack Magazine was the main outlet for the last French hackers who remained vocal. One exception was the creation of the *Misc Magazine*[26] by Frederic Raynal, known by the community as "pappy". Raynal adopted a professional perspective on hacking as soon as he graduated from its school of engineering in 1996, gaining his PhD in computer science in 2002, and launching Misc at the same time.[27] The magazine, contrary to the early e-zines from the 2000s, is publishing serious studies and code examples on topics such as rootkits, user space vulnerabilities, cryptography, and even research summaries on information warfare.[28] MISC contributed to diffuse a culture of computer security seen as a hobby in many French computer science and engineering schools. As computer sciences became an attractive option for many young French citizens, the casual and friendly reverse engineering practice became widely current in most schools, to the point of being taught and undertaken as student exercises in most French leading electrical and telecommunication engineering schools (e.g., Centrale-Supelec, ENST, Telecom Bretagne, etc.).

Meanwhile, preparation and sponsorship of large-scale attacks gained considerable traction as the core philosophy of hacking (based of freedom and activism values) was fading away with the diffusion of embedded cracking tools and libraries. Titan Rain (2003–2006) is an exemplar of these first explorations of cyber-warfare involving low-tech methodologies embedded into advanced campaigns (see Fig. 2.3). The earliest large-scale attacks emerged in 2000 with aggressive campaigning of Russian State sponsored hackers in the United States.[29] But Titan Rain was larger in scale and more systematic in its operating procedures. The original attacks were traced to the Chinese Province of Guandong, with an intensive use of persistent and advanced techniques. Titan Rain, for instance, was one of the first large-scale campaigns able to establish a large number of footholds by the rapid deployment of Remote Access Tools. As a campaign, Titan Rain gained access to many defense contractors' networks, including those of Lockheed Martin, Sandia National Laboratories, Redstone Arsenal, and NASA.

The first novelty introduced by Titan Rain lies in the intensive training received by the PLA Chinese core hacking group of 20 members. The attack first deployed a large reconnaissance campaign, and listed the most vulnerable networks belonging to the US Army (located at the Systems Engineering Command at Fort Huachuca,

---

[26]Misc Magazine http://www.miscmag.com. The publication contributed to the normalization and the acceptance of "cybersecurity" consultants in France. As humorously put by a French hacker, "Misc was surely the first technical magazine about computer security that you could read wearing a suit".

[27]http://www.miscmag.com.

[28]Fred Raynal is, in 2016, the very successful CEO of Quarkslab, a leading French cybersecurity consultancy firm of more than 50 employees. https://www.quarkslab.com.

[29]See Stoll (2000).

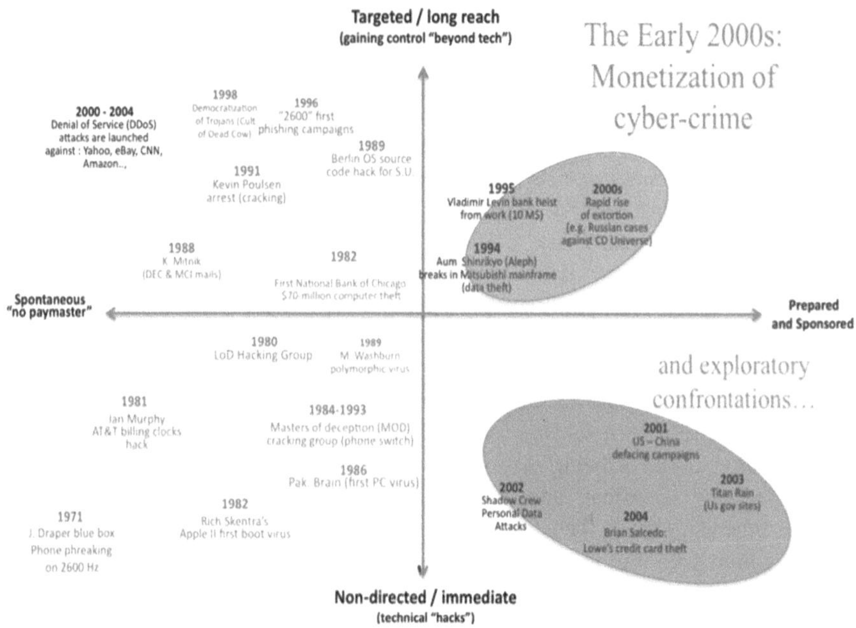

Fig. 2.3 The monetization of cyber-crime and first State confrontations

AZ). From a first foothold, the Chinese PLA unit moves on to grab hold of the Defense Information Systems Agency in Arlington, VA, less than 4 h after its first intrusion. During their first night of intruding US defense networks, the PLA group penetrated the Naval Ocean Systems Center in San Diego, CA, the US Army Space, and Strategic Defense installation in Huntsville, Alabama.[30]

Monetization of cyber-crime took many different forms. Some of these attacks were totally unprepared, immediate, non-directed, and rather successful. It is the case of the heist of Lowe's Hardware credit card system, hacked by Brian Salcedo through an unsecured wireless line in early 2003. Brian was just running around in his car with his best buddy in Michigan trying to find open wireless access, a fashionable activity for young geeks at the time. Salcedo discovered that the local Lowe's had not only an open access wireless, but that the network behind it was also unsecure. He took note of it. A few months later, he got back at it with a bunch of friends, and systematically, although carelessly, pawned, and juiced every single network layer he could access, day after day. As the local Police already knew Salcedo (from some rather brutal network intrusions), he decided to be more "stealth" this time, and planned in advance an escape route to Canada, then to

[30]Nathan Thornborough, "The Invasion of the Chinese Cyberspies (and the man who tried to stop them): An Exclusive Look at how the Hackers called TITAN RAIN are Stealing U.S. Secrets," Time Magazine, September 5, 2005 http://www.cs.washington.edu/education/courses/csep590/05au/readings/titan.rain.htm.

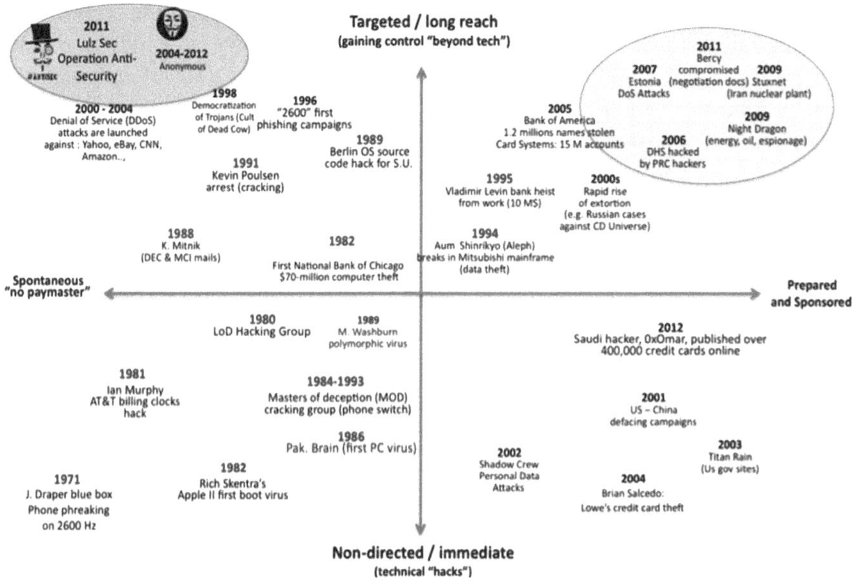

Fig. 2.4 Beyond technology: the rise of large-scale targeted campaigns (2005–2013)

Turkey, where he though there would be no extradition to the United States. Except that Salcedo used his Pontiac Grand Prix to do the heist, a car covered in hacker tags, and large antennas, that he parked not far away from the Lowe's. Salcedo and his three accomplices were caught in the act, sitting in their tacky Pontiac. The three accomplices were sentenced 1 year each, and Salcedo 9 years.[31] This case study became even more interesting when it was later discovered that Gonzalez, the man who blackmailed Salcedo in pursuing his hack as he was in the process of being caught, was in fact a FBI informant since 2003, who was actually paid $75,000 a year to set up and trick fellow hackers.[32]

In the Salcedo's case, this was a spontaneous, non-directed (a random store with weak protection) attack, which in fact has been prepared and *unknowingly* sponsored. The early 2000s are indeed the era of "stealth sponsorship". Many police enforcement agencies, in Europe and in the United States, got the green light to conduct sting operations in the cyber-space, including hiring hackers and former hackers; encouraging credit card thefts in order to catch hackers full-handed as it was already obvious that attribution and forensics would bring meager evidence in hacking and cracking cases.

[31]Read the retrospective story in Wired: Kevin Poulsen, «Indicted Federal Informant Allegedly Strong-Armed Hacker Into Caper That Drew 9-Year Sentence», 08/12/2008. https://www.wired.com/2008/08/indicted-federa/.

[32]https://www.wired.com/2010/03/gonzalez-salary/.

ShadowCrew is another exemplar of the ruthless imagination of the early 2000s. Kim Marvin, (known as "MacGyver"), Seth Sanders (known as Kidd), and Brett Johnson (known as Gollumfun) came up with the idea in 2002 of imitating the Amazon's business model for hacking.

The years 2005–2013 are marked by a double shift, and in some extent a seizure, between "target and sponsored campaigns" led by States or organized crime, and more pervasive "spontaneous and long-reach campaigns" led by activist groups, hackers' collectives, and loosely coupled entities such as Anonymous and LulzSec. This period is characterized by a rapid growth of strategic and politically motivated attacks (Kerem125 against the United Nations, Chinese APT1 global campaign, Estonia DoS attacks, Stuxnet, Operation Aurora, Fig. 2.4).

References

Ankara N (2007) A Personal view of the French underground 1992–2007. Phrack #64, 27 May 2007 http://phrack.org/issues/64/17.html

Baumard P (1991) Stratégie et surveillance des environnements concurrentiels. Masson, Paris

Clapes AL (1993) Softwars: the legal battles for control of the global software industry. Quorum Books, Westport, Conn

Guisnel J (1995) Guerres dans le cyberespace, La Découverte

Katie H, Markoff J (1995) Cyberpunk: outlaws and hackers on the computer frontier. Simon and Schuster, NY

Raymond ES (2000) A brief history of Hackerdom, Thyrsus Enterprises. http://www.catb.org/esr/writings/homesteading/hacker-history/

Sterling B (1994) Part three: law and order. The hacker crackdown: law and disorder on the electronic frontier. Bantam Books, New York

Stoll C (1988) Stalking the wily hacker. Commun ACM 31(5):484–500

Stoll C(1989) The cuckoo's egg: tracking a spy through the maze of computer espionage. DoubleBay, New-York

Stoll C (2000) The Cuckoo's Egg: Tracking a Spy Through the Maze of computer espionage. Simon and Shuster, NY

Warusfel B (2000) Contre-espionnage et protection du secret: Histoire, droit et organisation de la sécurité nationale en France. Panazol, Lavauzelle

Chapter 3
The Determinants of a National Cyber-Strategy

Abstract This chapter introduces the overarching framework in which each nation is developing its own cyber-security policy, and the unique position adopted by France in this landscape.

Keywords French politics · Cyber-defense · Cyber-security · Regulation · Nature of information · Political and geopolitical objectives of cyber-regulation · Counter-measures · False flags

3.1 The Nature of Information and Its Constraints on Regulation of Cyber-Defense

There is nothing more dangerous than to consider that information as binary and inert, such as the metaphor of a water molecule that would produce an ocean. The analogy of cyberspace with the maritime space indicates a profound lack of understanding of the cyber domain. To establish a national doctrine on such an analogy is preparing to lead the wrong war, and, more dramatically, to want to wage war on foundations that would only aggravate the vulnerability of the defense system.

Information is not inert. It cannot be taken for granted and cannot be assumed as a static element in policy.[1] The vision of knowledge as a stock is dangerous because it reduces the information as a static and inertial component of security and policy, enacting a policy void in cyberspace: devoid of values, giving undue weight to the logic of means. The strategic nature of information is not correlated with its novelty, the superiority of a technological breakthrough or its geographical origin.

Post-modern societies are highly dependent upon various forms of information, for most of their technical, societal, social and economic sub-systems are consuming as much information that they produce. The rise of machine intermediation has contributed to leave human sensemaking often in lag of speed, accuracy and

---

[1]Baumard (1994).

P. Baumard, *Cybersecurity in France*, SpringerBriefs in Cybersecurity,
DOI 10.1007/978-3-319-54308-6_3

pertinence. By 1999, most experts agreed that machine-to-machine communications could represent more than half of world traffic before the 2020s. This figure was reached in 2008. Information mostly circulates from machines to machines, from plane maintenance on board system to computers on the ground, from Internet servers to home desktops, from a financial transactions platform to a trader's desk.[2]

One consequence of such an acceleration of information diffusion lies into its autonomous development. Society and local organizations rarely possess the mechanisms to influence, forbid or shape its diffusion. While in legacy organizations, access to information is conditioned, and in turn shapes the societal strata of group and communities, information is now fairly accessible to everyone. The rise of electronic communications, and in particular of the internet in the late 1990s, has reduced the distance and privileges in accessing, producing, discussing or emitting information. Not only machines handle half of the world communication traffic, but also the other half suffers none or few deniability of access. While this status has produced tremendous learning opportunities for populations deprived of educational infrastructures, it has also produced a global network-centric society, relying on cyber-capabilities (critical infrastructures, energy supply, education, knowledge and health) and critically vulnerable to cyber-attacks.

The awareness of a new realm of attacks and vulnerabilities emerged in France with the Stuxnet campaign in 2010. In June of 2010, a malicious code was introduced in the software of a hardware component of the German firm Siemens intended to integrate the control and data acquisition system (SCADA) of a site of uranium enrichment at Natanz, Iran.[3] This malicious code exploited four vulnerabilities in Windows WinCC, which was still unaware of the existence (vulnerability called "zero day"). This malicious code established an external communication, as to trigger an instruction to paralyze them, and then sabotage the targeted nuclear installation. Although such an attack was not a first, and it had a few features that are not foreign in the wake of the international negotiations on the regulation of cyber-defense in general, and counter-measures, in particular. Stuxnet is what we call a campaign of advanced persistent threat (APT).

Such cyber-attacks are so named because they mimic the behavior of an intelligent and complex attack, with capabilities of reasoning and triggering stand-alone operations from a distance. Its characteristics are the behavioral programming of autonomous behaviors (their ability to adapt their attacks), their adaptability, and their persistence (after a period of recognition of their targets, they aim to compromise a system by living there, anonymously, or by deceiving the vigilance of the detection systems by increasing their privileges).

Stuxnet's goal was to reprogram, for purposes of sabotage, the logic controllers (PLCs) of the nuclear power plant. In particular, he was able to auto-replicate (by triggering its own installation from external removable media), to be run remotely

---

[2]See: Baumard (2010).

[3]Fallière et al. (2011).

through network sharing, to update by a peer-to-peer network, to take control of the command center, to hide its binary traces, to identify the security products residing on the network, edit them and then hide the sabotage codes directly on the industrial controllers (Plc) from Siemens.

This last characteristic, the auto replication associated with an astute elevation of privilege, is one of the causes of the great proliferation of Stuxnet, which infected nearly 100,000 machines from the day of its discovery (January 25, 2010, if we do not take into account the dormant versions in 2009), and by September 29, 2010, of which 14 industrial sites in Iran, and more than 60,000 hosts globally. By its magnitude, the sophistication of its construction, which was perceived as the sign the work of a State or of the cooperation between several States, Stuxnet was identified as the event starting the first global cyber-war.[4]

Stuxnet revealed the possibility of a global cyber-war, but it was, above all, a very effective demonstration of a systemic flaw in current network defense strategy: detection systems based on the identification of signatures of malicious code (tracking of malicious code in traffic) were ineffective in the face of intelligent attacks of this type and the degree of automation demonstrated by Stuxnet (which was spotted by a security company in Belarus because the machines did not stop reviving and updating!). The Stuxnet event shattered the sense of tranquility as to a "security and controlled" industrial era.[5] Schouwenberg, who was the head of the Kapersky team that contributed to defeat Stuxnet, was sincerely impressed by the elegance of its programming, which combined the operations crossroads of four "zero day" vulnerabilities.[6] The cyber-war became a reality, and its potential impact on cyber-space potentially displayed easily measurable societal implications and strategic implications. As in the fictional novel *The Opposing Shore* of Julien Gracq,[7] nothing gives more desire to men of war that a low signal-light on a distant shore.

This section of chapter 2 deals with the issue of the regulation and defense of national cyberspace that is, as we shall see, bound to become the heart of many conflicts (commercial, economic, armed) in the twenty-first century. In particular, this monograph addresses the strategy and organization of France national cyberdefense and cyber-strategy, and investigates the available strategic options to deploy national countermeasures against cyber attacks. Counter-measures are responses opposed to an attack or event so as to prohibiting, preventing or curbing its proliferation at its source. These three modes of responses (interdiction, prevention, deterrence) involve a very different posture. The *interdiction counter-measures* (type I) may simply end a malicious operation. In this scenario, security software would identify a malicious code, insulate it, place it in quarantine, and eventually remove it. *Preventive counter-measures* (type II) would characterize this malicious behavior (by its signature, its behavioral recognition) and ensure that it is stopped upon

[4]Farwell and Rohozinski (2011), and Lindsay (2013).

[5]Farwell and Rohozinski (2011), and Lindsay (2013).

[6]Kushner (2013).

[7]Julien Gracq, *Le Rivage des Syrtes*, Corti, 1951.

detection. The answers to Stuxnet fall into these first two categories. Finally, *proactive counter-measures* (type III) extend the temporary interdiction by an active search for its source of emission in order to proceed to its neutralization.

3.2 Building a National Strategy for Cyber-Defense

The mobility and pervasive nature of contemporary cyber-threats are most likely to defeat type I and type II counter-measures. Ending a cyber-attack campaign is likely to involve a retaliation that goes beyond its temporary interdiction, as most attacks would immediately morph into a new form, or a new source of emission. Attribution of the attack (the identification of its point of emission and emitter) would most likely involve a type III counter-measure, i.e. tracing and tracking the command and control of the attacker, wherever it might reside. Unfortunately, most modern attacks are transient to any geographical locations. Servers may be borrowed, and a complex transit strategy between hosts, countries, and *unaware* hosts is likely to characterize most advanced campaigns.

Counter-measures may be either led by software, or by human intervention, or more often composed of these two types of intervention. Counter-measure is therefore both a political decision and a set of lines of commands triggered from a detection system based on a programmed analytical reasoning (artificial intelligence, statistical correlation, Bayesian, etc.). Human counter-measures are carried out from investigation and survey (audit, forensics) by means that can be human (social engineering, interviews, under cover investigations) or computerized (reverse tracing of the path of attack, penetration tests, etc.). This second part may involve the tracing of the path of an attack that has passed through servers physically located in one or more foreign countries.[8]

This particular point has stalled global negotiations for a regulation of cybercrime, since its first initiative in Budapest on November 23, 2001. The Convention on Cybercrime, enacted through the Council of Europe, aimed at pursuing "as a matter of priority, a common criminal policy aimed at the protection of society against cybercrime, inter alia, by adopting appropriate legislation and fostering international co-operation". Whilst enacted in good faith, the Convention adopted very broad definitions of "data" and "information" that swiftly collided with sovereign interests of discussing parties. For instance, "traffic data" in the convention is defined as "computer data relating to a communication by means of a computer system, generated by a computer system that formed a part in the chain of communication, indicating the communication's origin, destination, route, time, date, size, duration, or type of underlying service".

This definition did not include any reservation, as to assess if the invoked data would contain sensitive or political information, trade secrets, and intellectual

[8]Talbot Jensen (2010).

property or would provide access to critical intelligence concerning its host. This first aspect triggered an immediate resistance of Russia and China, both countries refusing to make a distinction between "technical data" (such as computer data) and "information".[9] Hence, the Russian constitution itself does not discriminate between communication infrastructures, computer data and public information seen as a component of national sovereignty. The Article 32 of the Budapest convention, entitled "Trans-border access to stored computer data with consent or where publicly available" led the Convention to a state of permanent stall, that is still lasting in 2017. This article states: "A Party may, without the authorization of another Party: (a) access publicly available (open source) stored computer data, regardless of where the data is located geographically; or (b) access or receive, through a computer system in its territory, stored computer data located in another Party, if the Party obtains the lawful and voluntary consent of the person who has the lawful authority to disclose the data to the Party through that computer system".

This article 32 raises several issues that led to its procedural inefficiency, and the impossibly to reasonably enforce it without breaching domestic sovereignty frameworks. Its first part, i.e. "accessing publicly available (open source) computer data" raises no particular issues, as an open source data, given it is available with adequate licenses (e.g. creative commons) is accessible regardless of domestic legal limitations. It would be dubious and very improbable that any sensitive hacking material, with interest for a nation-state, would be made publicly available through an open source license; even if most ethical hacking research, both defensive and "attack research" are indeed publicly available.

The second part, i.e. "(b) access or receive, through a computer system in its territory, stored computer data located in another party" is more problematic. Randomly accessing data in foreign computer storage equates with violating the right of privacy of individuals, the right of a citizen to defend its presumed innocence, the right of a legal representation, and ultimately, the territorial and legal sovereignty of a foreign state. If the text assumes preexistent and ongoing police cooperation between nation-states, led in particular within the framework of Interpol, the text does not precise how this existing framework would be actionable within the proposed Article 32 of the Budapest convention. A "lawful authority" triggers, moreover, additional causal ambiguity as the adjective lawful may relate to a domestic legitimacy in one of the territorial parties, but the lawfulness of investigation greatly varies between nations and territories.

Several variables are essential to understand the obstacles to international cooperation in cyberdefense and cybersecurity. The first one is attribution. Most experts would enthusiastically states that *attribution is easy*. Attribution is easy within the "*known unknows*", i.e. when attackers are adopting pattern and techniques that have been previously used (signatures); when attackers are careless, i.e. when they did not take the cautious steps for hiding their identity; and when there is a robust and non truncated chain of evidence between the point of origin of the

---

[9]Fleck (2012).

attack campaign and its outcome. These idealistic conditions are rarely met. Most attackers have the required skills to construct variations of preexisting techniques. Such variations are keyboard strokes away from the original malware. An inexperienced hacker may create poor variations of used malwares; but even if the hypothesis of an amateurish variation of existing code, the outcome would only inform that elements of known attacks (e.g. FancyBear, Duke, APT28, etc.) have been recorded and recombined. Would it robustly inform of the attacker's point of origin, nationality or geographical location? No. Anyone can access, buy, or develop a malevolent code that is inspired by an existing Chinese, American or Russian code, without this recombination being an evidence of its author's nationality or geographical location. Consequently, an error of attribution is very likely and may create a false flag that would undoubtedly trigger an undesired escalation of conflict.

Another dire aspect of attribution is that attribution may be revealing. An attribution work may disclose the level of skills and knowledge of the auditor. If attribution fails, then the attacker knows that his skillfulness is much higher than the defender's skill set. Even if attribution succeeds, it will very precisely inform the attacker of the level of knowledge that the defender possesses. The bottleneck of the attribution lies in identifying malevolent code, indicators of compromise (IOC). Here, the defender has two options. On one hand, the defender can reveal the IOCs, malware, malevolent codes that were found after auditing the code. If the defender reveals only these IOCs or malware, he or she would have to reveal how precisely this code was implemented, used, articulated into an attack campaign. Reveal how an attack campaign has been implement would ultimately reveal the strengths and weaknesses of the defense line, which is, understandably, inconceivable for a sovereign nation-state, as well as it would be for a corporation (Table 3.1).

3.2.1 Anonymity, Attribution and Evidence of Intentionality

On December 12, 2016, Jean-Yves Le Drian, France's Minister of Defense, introduced the new French national cyberdefense doctrine. This new national cyber-defense doctrine enacted cyber-defense as an "art of war", i.e. the use of electronic and computing capabilities for the pursuit of war will no longer be considered as an under-specialization. Specifically, this reform meant that cyber-defense would become in France an independent military domain, with its own ranks, martial ecology, doctrines, teaching and command. It also meant that France would shift from a technical and passive defense philosophy in the cyber domain (reinforced vertical and sovereign systems, data storage and isolated networks), towards a dynamic and active defense; i.e. including an active use of the three types of countermeasures: preventive, coercive and proactive. A proactive countermeasure doctrine involves legitimating the use of systematic retaliation when attribution has been established; and when national and sovereign assets are

Table 3.1 Determinants and outcomes of attack attribution

Determinants	Risks	Obstacles	Outcomes
Attribution (identifying the attacker)	– False-flag or error of attribution may escalate an unjustified conflict – Attributing an attack is revealing the level of competency of the auditor	– *Network* and *code* cross boundaries and impede national sovereignty – Unwillingness of disclosing own capabilities by disclosing indicators of compromise (need to know)	– Budapest convention signed but not ratified – Absence of communal international legal framework to fight transnational cybercrime
Constant morphing of attack codes	– Errors in attribution and accountability – False negatives – Usage of a malevolent code does not systematically correlates with authorship or territorial origin	– Geography of the command and control (C&C) of attacker is not an evidence of attack's emitter's own geographical location – Geographical tags can be easily tempered, morphed and be produced as false flags	– Attack campaigns will always outpace defense, and its legal frameworks – A signature is not a solid legal evidence of authorship – Morphing attacks can erase their traces
Automated AI-assisted proliferation (artificial intelligence)	– Statistical correlation does not establish causality or point of origin – Ubiquity of peer-to-peer architectures makes it impossible to identify an origin of code creation	– A pattern of attacks can be manufactured, even on a very large scale – Patterns taken by bots are unpredictable – Network capacities and bandwidth are likely to have been borrowed by attackers	– Autonomous development of an AI-driven cyber-martial ecology – Attribution and gain chains are obfuscated and impenetrable

being compromised and duly threatens the security and safety of the French population.[10]

In his announcement, the French Minister of Defense, Jean-Yves Le Drian, introduced the two "renewed" and central concepts of the French national cyberdefense doctrine: "riposte" (*retaliation*) and "neutralization". Under the new doctrine, "riposte" (retaliation) would be considered legitimate and immediate in case of an immediate threat for the national security of French citizens, life-supporting infrastructures ("of vital interest"), that may encompass a wide variety of archetypes, ranging for nuclear installations, railroads, hospitals, etc. Immediate retaliation would encompass the potential use of remote access tool as to search and destroy aggressive and distant capabilities, even if they reside in a

[10]«Comment Le Drian crée une cyber-armée française», *Challenges*, 13/12/2016. http://www.challenges.fr/entreprise/defense/comment-le-drian-cree-une-cyber-armee-francaise_442784.

foreign territory (ibid.). The Minister of Defense added in the public introduction of the new doctrine that escalation models from strategic, kinetic and cyberwarfare would be permeable; i.e. that a conventional kinetic retaliation may be used in case of a large scale cyber-attack. While seeming softer, "neutralization" would involve the delay (work factor, slowing or paralyzing opponents) or the stopping of a cyber campaign (malware deployment, intrusions) as to safeguard the national stability and safety of the public.

This new French national cyberdefense doctrine is very similar, in its enactment of a "cyber-sovereignty", with the national doctrines of Russia and the People Republic of China. It suffers from the exact same legal and philosophical imperfections. On the legal arena, a sovereign State that would engage offensive and military capabilities on the physical territory of another sovereign State would evidently breach every principle of international humanitarian law. "Neutralizing" a computing, software, electronic or signal distant capability involves a "hack back", i.e. a forceful entry into a foreign or distant system (when this system is in space or in international waters). Such a forceful entry would not only breach privacy and private property laws, and be considered a theft or violation of property; it would also be considered an act of foreign aggression if this "distant asset" or "aggressing entity" eventually reveals itself as being a foreign State property. The problem with an offensive and retaliating cyberdefense doctrine is always the same corner stone: *the reliability of attribution.*

On one hand, it is difficult to establish an a priori criminal destination of an information system, or information itself. For example, the use of secret and encryption can be a guarantee for the respect of individual freedom and anonymity as well as the sign of a criminal activity. In fact, whistleblowers are using the same technologies as criminal organizations to communicate and to exchange anonymous data (e.g. Tor network). The "cyber-libertarian", the "whistleblower", the "resistant", the "rebel" or the "cyber-terrorist" are often one and the same person depending on whether they are perceived from a different side of the fence.

While the creation or the possession of a malicious code may qualify as an evidence of a malevolent intent, advanced cyber-attack campaigning may not involve any malicious code, but rather rely on the extraordinary talent of the attacker: a command line used on a network is not a priori a weapon. The combination of legit and benign lines of code may, in the realm of cyber-security, become a powerful weapon, with or *without* the use of malicious codes. Hence, in the pioneering spirit of hacking, a genuine hacker was praised for his or her ability to defeat a system or a network defense by means of astute learning, and *not* thorough cracking or brute force. Furthermore, encryption is so freely available that the audit work and scientific investigation of a complex code can take several weeks. A functional approach and typological characterization of "offensive criminal information" is thus doomed to failure.[11]

---

[11]Talbot Jensen (2010)

On the other hand, the architecture of information systems, for reasons of efficiency, is not delimited by its ends, but by the performance of operations that can be distributed, shared, or randomly "sparsed" within peer-to-peer architectures. Therefore, the geography of information, its destination as well as its source, becomes the result of a process that will allow, —whether intentionally or not—, hiding its origin, its purpose, its chronology and its owner.

The difficulty lies in the interpretation of the responsibility of the different stakeholders (telecom operators, States, software manufacturers, etc.) in the final expression that can result from these complex information pathways.[12] In the article 32 of the Budapest convention (2001), the obligation of information disclosure lies in the domestic legal authority; but as attribution is most likely impossible to establish ex ante, most cyber-cooperation faces the obstacle of establishing the determinacy and attribution of attacks.[13]

The Budapest Convention on cyber crime, since 2001, has been signed by 60 countries; but, according to the UNODC, only a third of the world population in a situation of connectivity, and a forecast of connectivity to 70% of the planetary population in 2017, the question of "counter-measures" and the authority to lead, is a challenge that goes well beyond the issue of cross-border cooperation. On one hand, with more than 90% of global communications in 2015 as machine-to-machine without human intermediation, it can be dangerous, from the point of view of the simple effectiveness of the Law, to assign to adopt a legal framework that takes human intent and attribution for granted, discarding the automation, artificial intelligence and robotic nature of most modern attacks.

On the other hand, the speed of the micro transactions, the speed with which an attack can be transformed into a sixty of its variants, do not leave a reasonable advance to legislature, the executive and law enforcement. That leaves law enforcement in the narrow and improbable scope of catching a cyber-criminal with weapons *at hand*.

While finding attack ex post evidence on a server may not be a difficult task, detecting and arresting a cyber-theft in real time is altogether another realm. Moreover, revealing and sharing attackers' intelligence may inform the attackers on the robustness of the defense; the disclosure itself has a low probability of being judicially actionable.[14]

Whether in Europe, the United States, Russia, China, Africa, or Brazil, few cases of "cyber-crimes" are effectively treated by the judicial system, and much less have been sanctioned. The mechanisms of judicial co-operation are very often ineffective in the areas of cybercrime, not through a lack of talent,—as State forces usually have decisive talents in this area—but by the unworkable nature of the technical co-operation on cybercrime.[15]

[12]Van Eeten al. (2011).

[13]Kenneth (2010).

[14]Kenneth (2010).

[15]Fleck (2012).

Sharing a "case" of cybercrime means sharing a vulnerability of its system of defense, as most advanced attacks are also significantly at the border of radical innovation. Therefore, if a State is cooperating with another, it will likely refuse to comply sharing "zero day" attacks (attacks in which the fault has not been previously identified), for fear of revealing to other States its state of the art, its real degree of mastery of the cyber-defense, or even a flaw that could be exploited for other purposes (espionage, cyber-war).

A "zero-day" is just as much vulnerability when publicly disclosed, as an opportunity for conducting offensive campaigns against allies and foes. Executive decision is hence in a permanent prisoner's dilemma: saying too much would impede national discretion about capabilities, while saying too little puts the defensive system at risk of ignoring a threat that has been underestimated. Critical flaws, in the cyber realm, are *weapons*.

As each actor seeks to create decisive asymmetries—facing of foreign powers that are not always benevolent—, there is no incentive to disclose information on this type of vulnerabilities. Therefore, in the current state of affairs, responding to an attack is a difficult political choice, especially when the attack campaign is cross-border. Cross-border access to data is difficult. It is not a question of the attack data itself (logs, IOCs), but more critically the necessity to *put it into context* to make it credible.

3.2.2 *Attribution of Democratic National Committee's Russian Intrusion*

This bottleneck of attribution was particularly salient in the case of the alleged intrusion of Russian hackers into the Democratic National Committee during the US presidential election campaign. The events, reported by Crowdstrike, unfolded as follows: "On June 15, 2016 a blog post to a WordPress site authored by an individual using the moniker Guccifer 2.0 claimed credit for breaching the Democratic National Committee".[16] This event triggered the interest of most cybersecurity specialists, and led to an active quest for a credible attribution of the attack. Three of these firms, SecureWorks, Fidelis and Crowdstrike became very active in establishing a credible attribution scenario for the attacks.

The three firms collected evidence with the cooperation of the DNC that granted access to their servers to search for indicators of compromise. Several IOCs were found, in the form of hashes of very well known hacking toolkits. Two of them in particular were of special interest: CrowdStrike found IOCs indicating that hackers used malware codes belonging to two malware sets from APT28 and APT29: Fancy Bear and Cozy Bear.

[16]Alperovitch (2016).

Fancy Bear is a hacking group producing a set of spear phishing tools that had been previously used in the Pawn Storm campaign, "active economic and political cyber-espionage operation that targets a wide range of entities, like the military, governments, defense industries, and the media".[17] The malware was an iOS7 app that ran in the background of Iphone operating systems, collecting contact lists, location data, capable of voice recording and sending out the WiFi status of the infected terminal. Three hashes of the compromised files were generated and made available.[18]

The specific tool used by the Operation Pawn Storm is X-Agent, and is reputably one of the many productions of the Fancy Bear group. As noted by Dmitri Alperovitch, Fancy Bear "has a wide range of implants at their disposal, which have been developed over the course of many years and include Sofacy, X-Agent, X-Tunnel, WinIDS, Foozer and DownRange droppers, and even malware for Linux, OSX, IOS, Android and Windows Phones. This group is known for its technique of registering domains that closely resemble domains of legitimate organizations they plan to target. Afterwards, they establish phishing sites on these domains that spoof the look and feel of the victim's web-based email services in order to steal their credentials. FANCY BEAR has also been linked publicly to intrusions into the German Bundestag and France's TV5 Monde TV station in April 2015".[19]

The problem is that most criminal hacking groups are developing hacking tools for *profit*. Many of the mentioned tools are widely available for download and execution from open sources; and could also be acquired within a "package plan", which includes monitoring, maintenance, training and updates. Owning or renting a Russian weapon does not mean that the owner or the renter is Russian. Otherwise the world Russian population would dramatically increase if each owner of a Kalashnikov would gain immediate Russian nationality.

The other indicators of compromise unveiled by Crowdstrike and SecureWorks indicated that toolkits from another group, Cozy Bear, had also been used. Much less is known about "Cozy Bear". According to Crowdstrike, the Cozy Bear hacking group is composed of Russian nationals working for, or working with, the Russian intelligence services.[20] The problem is that names of hackers' groups are often simply given by security analysts. So CozyBear also goes by the names of the Dukes (given by Volexity), the Office Monkeys, CozyCar or CozyDuke (given by F-Secure). The NCCIC and the FBI came up with their own name for the very same

[17] Sun et al. (2015).

[18] The hashes were 05298a48e4ca6d9778b32259c8ae74527be33815; 176e92e7cfc0e57be83e-901c36ba17b255ba0b1b; 30e4decd68808cb607c2aba4aa69fb5fdb598c64.

[19] D. Alperovitch, ibid.

[20] Early US governmental attributions were specifically pointing the GRU, the intelligence wing of the Russian Army. Cf. Shaun Walker, "US Expulsions put spotlight on Russia's GRU Intelligence Agency", *The Guardian*, December 30, 2016. However, a definitive attribution concerning either GRU of FSB was never established.

group: Grizzly Steppe.[21] An obvious second obstacle for rigorous attribution: names of hacking groups are the result of creative thinking and imaginative capabilities of every single private or governmental organizations, which (a) want to claim the paternity of their identification; (b) want to convey a commercial or political message; and (c) without any consideration for the actual authorship of the group of tools they may put together in the "attribution basket". No one really knows the real name of "CozyBear" or "FancyBear", and no one really knows if these are actually human groups, which from the organizational theorist point of view are defined by an ensemble of human beings who regularly interact in order to pursue a common goal.

For the NCCIC, both CozyBear and FancyBear are subdivisions of Russian intelligence services, greatly simplifying the debate by merging all assumptions in one very simple attribution: "The U.S. Government confirms that two different RIS actors participated in the intrusion into a U.S. political party. The first actor group, known as Advanced Persistent Threat (APT) 29, entered into the party's systems in summer 2015, while the second, known as APT28, entered in spring 2016".[22] The NCCIC and the FBI may confuse the public. They picked the names of attack campaigns (APTs) to name their groups. In that domain, the French intelligence services showed far greater creativity in naming hackers groups and hacking tools: Babar, Barbapapa, Asterix, a.k.a. the whole catalog of traditional French comics.[23] COZY BEAR (APT29)'s favorite intrusion technique is a targeted spearphish campaign that usually consists of an e-mail message pointing to a web link that silently inject a malicious dropper in the victim's operating system.[24] In the DNC case, this e-mail invited John Podesta, the then chairman of the 2016 Hillary Clinton presidential campaign, to renew the password of his Google account. Despite a common sense rule that is widely shared among the general public, John Podesta, after asking the security administrator if the e-mail was legitimate, simply clicked on the weblink and triggered both the injection and the release of his personal password to adversaries (Fig. 3.1).

The basic phishing technique used by CozyBear is not particularly innovative. The same technique is found in most recent APT campaign tools, including APT30 (based on CozyDuke) that has been attributed to the Chinese's PLA. Once the target fell in the phishing trap, which in return runs an executable (either locally once injected, or from a distant C&C (command and control).

Once inside, the software agent moves laterally to install either a backdoor or a dropper. In a backdoor scenario, attackers gain a persistent access to the infected machines, which is the most probable scenario in the DNC case. Eventually, a

---

[21]"Grizzly Steppe: Russian Malicious Cyber Activity", NCCIC – FBI Joint Analysis Report, N° JAR-16-20296, December 29, 2016 https://www.us-cert.gov/sites/default/files/publications/JAR_16-20296A_GRIZZLY%20STEPPE-2016-1229.pdf.

[22]NCCIC-FBI joint report analysis, op. cit., p. 2.

[23]Franceschi-Bicchierai (2015).

[24]D. Alperovitch, ibid.

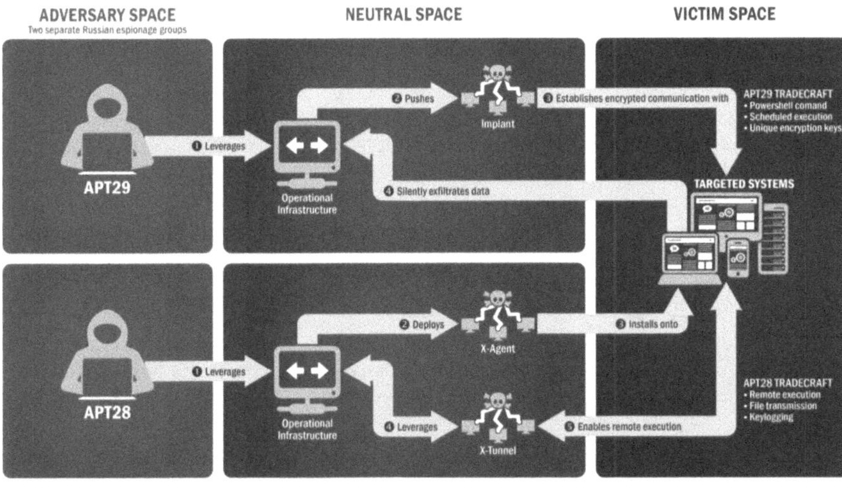

Fig. 3.1 Techniques used by APT29 and APT28 (*Source* NCCIC, 2016)

dropper, i.e. a resident software component allowing the silent downloading of additional hacking tools to the targeted system, may also be implanted. Additional tools may include executable codes that archive and then send out sensitive information; a data exfiltration module connected to an external server; a secure file deletion module; and eventually, an impersonator and key generator to alter or elevate privileges. The security solutions vendors' story would be perfect attribution *bravado* if it were real and credible.

The most damaging evidence against a Russian attribution came from WordFence in a blog entry from December 30, 2016. When analyzing the NCCIC-FBU Joint-Report, WordFence discovered that the PHP malware indicators of compromise (IOC) unveiled in the FancyBear exploit. WordFence extracted the incriminated code, and ran it in a sandbox to observe its actual behavior. They note: "By viewing the source code, we could find the name of the malware and the version. It is P.A.S. 3.1.0."[25] The problem is that P.A.S. 3.1.0. is an outdated version of this malware, that had reached version 4.1.1 in December 2016.

Twelve generations of code in a malware indicate that a tool may itself suffer critical vulnerabilities, as hacking tools need also to be up to date to avoid hack back, detection or even a reverse compromise. It is very unlikely that any government would use a very outdated version of a hacking tool, not because they would try to avoid detection (sometimes, "signing" an attack can be an intentional warning to adversaries); but to avoid providing a real evidence of an act of war. On an older and less secure generation of a hacking tool, evidence could be obtained on the real point of the origin of the attack, and then brought to international court, or

[25]Maunder (2016).

Table 3.2 Attribution analysis of the DNC case

Evidence (IOCs)	Attribution rationale	Causal ambiguity
Disclosure of discovered hashes (SHA256) of FancyBear and CozyBear malware tools[a]	Using a malware toolbox that is reputably attributed to two Russian hacking groups (APT28 and APT29)	The tools are widely available and any hacker can use them, making it possible to anyone to impersonate APT28 or APT29
The same hacking tools were used to infect Ukrainian artillery via an App named Попр-Д30.apk[b]	Defeating Ukrainian artillery is a Russian benefit, which indicates that APT29 is a FSB or GRU tool[c]	Copy and incorporation of X-Agent is common in many hacking tools, outside of the APT 29 realm
FancyBear and CozyBear executables found on DNC servers	Presence of tools is sufficient evidence for the Russian destination of the breach	No evidence was disclosed concerning how, when and to which IP addresses data were transferred[d]

[a]See bottom page of Crowdstrike report: https://www.crowdstrike.com/blog/bears-midst-intrusion-democratic-national-committee/
[b]FancyBear was used to inject a malware in a targeting application used by Ukrainian military personnel using Soviet-era D-30 Howitzers. See Crowdstrike's report, December 22, 2016, "Use of Fancy Bear Android malware in tracking of Ukrainian field artillery units", https://www.crowdstrike.com/wp-content/brochures/FancyBearTracksUkrainianArtillery.pdf
[c]See http://www.forbes.com/sites/thomasbrewster/2016/12/22/android-howitzer-app-gru-hac-of-dnc-russian-link-crowdstrike/#431fb7f82f03
[d]G. Eliason, "Why Crowdstrike's Russian hacking story fell apart – Say hello to FancyBear", Whashinton Post Blog, January 3, 2017 http://www.washingtonsblog.com/2017/01/crowdstrikes-russian-hacking-story-fell-apart-say-hello-fancy-bear-2.html

the UN Security Council in that matter. Alas, several critical flaws can be identified in this attribution case. We list them in the Table 3.2.

The second problem with the identification of P.A.S. 3.1.0 in the Joint Report is that this tool is not Russian, but Ukrainian, as the screenshot provided by WordFence clearly shows (see screenshot Fig. 3.2).

The third problem with this evidence is that P.A.S. is a very successful hacking tool for compromising PHP-based website (and the actual motivation of WordFence to defend their business model, as this security firm provides security services for WordPress customers). As noted by WordFence, "DHS provided us with 876 IP addresses as part of the package of indicators of compromise. Lets look at where they are located. The chart (Fig. 3.3) shows the distribution of IP addresses by country".[26] The table below shows the IP addresses distribution of usage.

When WordFence analyzed who were the actual owners of these global IP addresses, they discovered a very fragmented ownership. Among the top three owners, OVH SAS, a French web hosting and server provider, was displaying 36 occurrences of hosting the malware. The explanation is that most of the top hosters

[26]M. Maunder, op. cit.

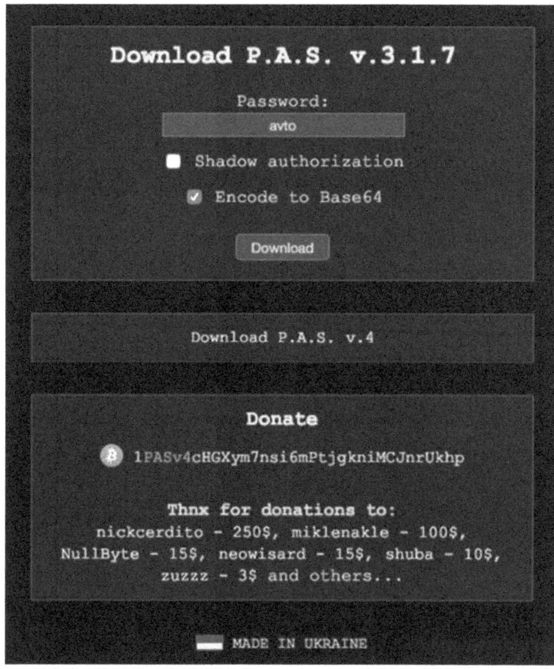

Fig. 3.2 P.A.S. 3.1.7. screenshot (*Source* WordFence)

of the malware toolkit were very well known hosting companies, such as Digital Ocean, Linode, Hetzner and OVH. As Maunder (ibid.) notes: "A common pattern that we see in the industry is that accounts at these hosts are compromised and those hacked sites are used to launch attacks around the web".

This discovery led Maunder to an evident conclusion: "The malware sample is old, widely used and appears to be Ukrainian. It has no apparent relationship with Russian intelligence and it would be an indicator of compromise for any website." (ibid.).

The fourth problem with this attribution case is that absolutely none contextual information is provided concerning the APT28 and APT29 operations. As noted by William Binney, the designer of the NSA global surveillance system, "I expected to see the IP's or other signatures of APT's 28/29 [the entities which the U.S. claims hacked the Democratic emails] and where they were located and how/when the data got transferred to them from DNC/HRC [i.e. Hillary Rodham Clinton]/etc. They seem to have been following APT 28/29 since at least 2015, so, where are they?"[27]

The DNC hacking case is an archetype of the obstacles met when resolving a cyber conflict. Even if the US Department of Homeland Security had contextual evidence, it could hardly disseminate it, because knowing the IP addresses, or the

[27]"Creator of NSA's Global Surveillance System Calls B.S. on Russian Hacking Report", *Washington Blog*, December 30, 2016 http://www.washingtonsblog.com/2016/12/creator-nsas-global-surveillance-system-calls-b-s-russian-hacking-report.html.

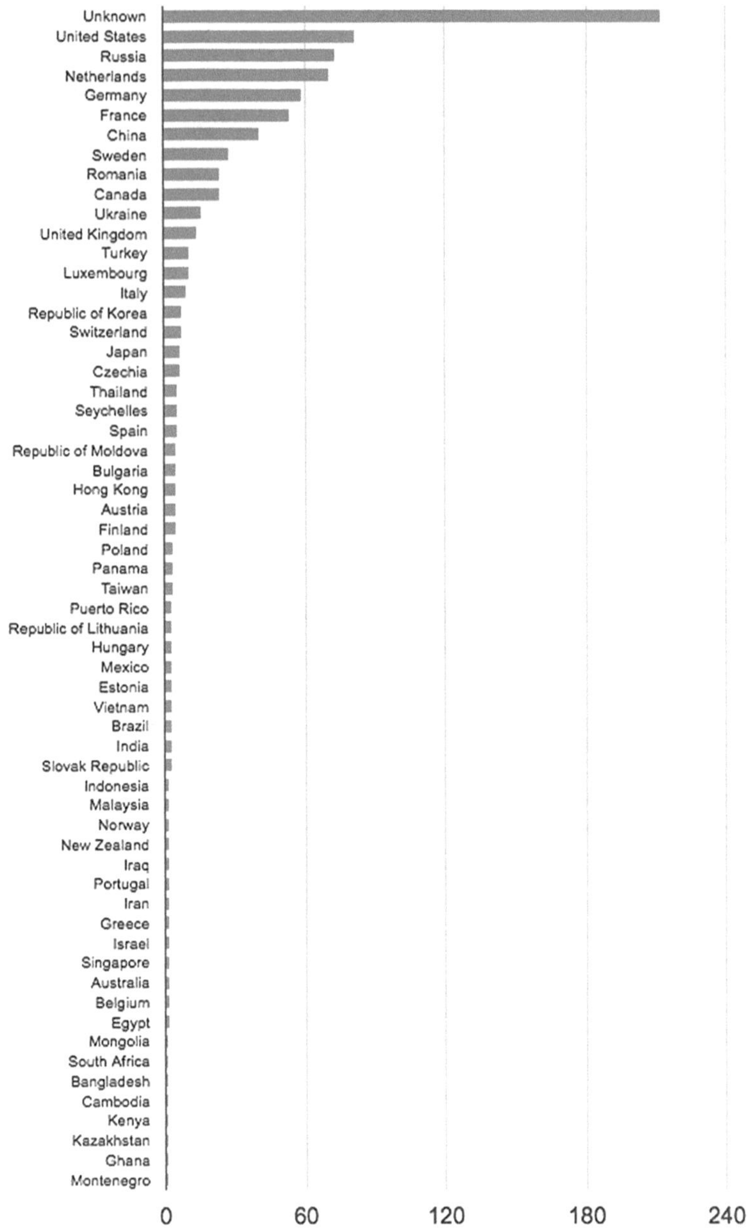

Fig. 3.3 Analysis of IP addresses used by P.A.S (*Source* DHS and DNI)

location, of an adversary's cyberwarfare unit is a strategic advantage. Losing this key advantage on the sake of establishing irrefutable evidence of an intrusion may not be worthy. The reality of cyberwarfare is that most hosts belong to the "unknown" category (see above figure). Malware can proliferate through Tor networks, transit through borrowed or stolen hosting services (the OVH case), and use chunks of codes that belong to many different hacking sets, from different nationalities. The nationality itself of the producer of the hacking tools is not an indicator of the sponsor, as criminal hacking activities reside in countries with the sole criteria of escaping or corrupting the Police. Ukraine, Turkey, Albania, but also Italy, France, Germany and the United States are excellent candidates for this criterion for different reasons. Undoubtedly, Russia excels in cyberwarfare and is a probable candidate for several politically motivated cyber campaigns. But so is everyone else.

3.2.3 Cyber Domain Definition: A "Political" Ontology

Nation-States do not share a common ontology when it comes to the definition of information commons, privacy, and sovereignty. France, in that matter, cultivates a paradox between the defense of civil liberties and a ubiquitous State, proliferating rules, regulations and control. On one hand, France enforced gradual control of copyright infringement with its Hadopi legislation, which enforces the law through direct interception of Internet traffic of citizens, with the cooperation of Internet service providers. On the other hand, France's National Assembly showed support for the legalization of an Edward Snowden-inspired whistle-blowing legal framework through amendments in April 2015, and swiftly denounced US abuse of telecommunication interceptions, following Edward Snowden revelations. Accordingly, France tends to share the perspective of opponents of the Tallinn Manual when it comes to the definition of territorial integrity: operations that "neither cause physical damage nor amount to an intervention nevertheless violates targeted state's sovereignty".[28] The international group of experts, indeed, never reached consensus.

Likewise, Russia and China share a similar perspective on sovereignty, more in that matter by fear of seeing a "rule of proportionality", as suggested by the Tallinn Manual,[29] to become a new international framework for conflict engagement. Both parties have bluntly rejected the Tallinn's proposition that suggests "a victim state is entitled to take proportionate measures to end harmful ongoing cyber operations if the state of origin fails to meet its obligation to end them".[30] The idea that such a position may harvest "*cyber sanctuaries*" for rogue cyber-activities has also been declined as irresolvable, as the share understanding, amongst opponents of the Tallinn Manual and the Budapest Convention is that both initiatives pursue a strategic objective of "softening" national defenses in the interest of the United

[28]Schmitt (2014).
[29]Schmitt (2013).
[30]M.N. Schmitt, op. cit, p. 277.

States. Most criminal cyber-campaigns are launched from countries where organized crime considers itself safe from police intervention: with weaker extradition laws, large and available (a.k.a. unsecure) high bandwidth capabilities. Origins of attack hence follow the best available path to maximize these three criteria, and statistics about origins of attack are not telling much about the country's involvement in cyber offensive campaigns.

The tensions experienced during the international negotiations for a regulation of cyber-defense are mostly anchored in the causal ambiguities, and the strategic risks, associated with attribution. The Budapest convention of November 2001, which actually aimed at regulating cybercrime, has still not been ratified by China and Russia in January 2017. And the core issue that blocks these negotiations is the definition of the cyber-domain: what can be considered as a risk for the stability of nations (and may be shared through adequate police or defense cooperation), and what is considered as a constitutional element of people's right to privacy and national sovereign domain.

On one side, most historical G8 nations separate cyber crime (i.e. the fight against crime in cyberspace), cyber-defense (i.e. strategic actions of the States in the middle of it) and cyber security (encouraged by the manufacturers, who hope a regulatory framework to be laid out). On the other, the Russians have long defended that these notions do not exist individually, but that there is a single and complete "information security", including both the container and the content.[31] All regulatory initiatives have pretended to ignore the obstacle, until the last initiative to establish a common glossary in 2014. But the Russians or the Chinese could not renounce their respective constitutional commitments, which perceive information as a sanctuary for sovereignty, both as a mass media and governmental prerogative, and *not* perceived as a neutral and normative technical platform.

Nothing, however, suggested that the rules of engagement and the legitimacy of cyberwar would be permanently transformed by the advent of a digital society. As Goldsmith points out, no one in the first decade of the existence of the "network of networks" has ever been concerned with security issues. Until 1988, when Robert Tappan Morris, a student at Cornell, introduced a worm into the internet emerging in which the experimental aim was to measure the size of the network, and eventually put out of use 10% of the 60,000 machines that made up the net. It is in 1988, that was born the first official program of DARPA on the security of the networks, with as a perspective, the resilience of the scenarios of attacks on the infrastructure…

---

[31]The renewed Doctrine of Information Security, enacted by Russian President Vladimir Putin on December 5, 2016, reinforced this perspective. In the renewed doctrine, information security is defined as follows: "the state of security of the person, society and the state from internal and external information threats, which provide realization of constitutional rights and freedoms of man and citizen, decent quality and standard of living citizens, sovereignty, territorial integrity and sustainable socio-economic development of the Russian Federation, and the defense State security".

Berlin was the place where the real issues of cyber security crystallized around the "Hagbard" case, a pseudonym for Kar Werner Koch, and the birth of the Chaos Computer Club in 1981 around Markus Hess, Hans Heinrich Hübner or Otto Brezinski. The misuse of technology is inseparable from the pursuit of a political goal, and therefore, for the Russians as for the Americans, who are competing in the first cyber-war around the fall of the Berlin Wall. The digital space was already a field of geopolitical conflict.

If the political purpose of a destabilization campaign is not difficult to establish, at least a posteriori, it is very difficult to define what constitutes an "act of war" from the point of view of cybernetics. The Chaos Computer Club, from its foundation, pursued the objective of demonstrating of the potential dangers of misuse of information technologies for the freedom of expression, individual liberty and democracy, invited itself into the political debate by technical prowess. These demonstrations were numerous between 1981 and 2013. The most symbolic CCC operation was the hack that demonstrated the ease with which a small group could intercept voting machines in less than three minutes.[32] Carried out in 2006, in cooperation with a Dutch foundation for the freedom of the individual, this exploit of the CCC has led to a revision of the constitutional court of the Netherlands the supervision of the electronic voting, and then to the abandonment of electronic voting. It is understandable, therefore, that we can't blindly apply preconceived framework to the public law or private law, in the cyber-domain without taking a few precautions. Should we judge the action of the CCC under the angle of the common law, and therefore, prohibit and sanction from its first steps? Or, should we judge it by its purpose of "whistleblower", and therefore, acknowledge the nobility of its purpose?

3.2.4 The Impact of Cybersecurity's Causal Ambiguities on National Policies

The first ambiguity of the exercise of judgment on a computer crime resides in its *ex-ante* "non-determinacy". The CCC operation demonstrated that the manipulation of voting machines could have easily been conducted by a criminal organization with the purpose of manipulating the results of a national vote. The vector itself cannot be a priori typified as an evidence of malicious intent. Many hacks do not involve the use of a malicious code. Many system flaws can be exploited without breaking any secure code.

A code does not carry *intentionality*.[33] While *cracking* may heavily rely on illegal and criminal toolkits, *hacking* can be the outcome of extraordinary talent,

[32]Bart and Pieters (2009).

[33]This statement underlines the versatility of coding. A harmless set of instructions can carry a high degree of malevolence if place in another context, or another level of privilege. There are, of course, instructions that are per se harmful.

using what has been left opened for exploitation.[34] Before even being able to identify the perpetrator of a computer crime ("attribution"), it is difficult to establish the actual intent of a reconnaissance, the usage of a hacking tool (that can be used for research purposes), or simply judging that exceptional talent is a marker of criminal intention (for white hackers).

Thus, approaches that want to a priori characterize actors in the cyberspace as "wicked" or "well-intentioned" denote both a great naiveté and lack of knowledge of the subject. They constitute nothing else than an attempt to promote a form of *"digital prima facie tort"* in the regulatory framework.

The second ambiguity lies in the *teleology* of computer crimes: malware proliferate in a "neutral space" before reaching their targets. This neutral space is composed of all the servers, hosting services, individual computer networks, university networks, public servers that malevolent hacking groups may borrow to conduct their cyber campaigns. Most of these "transit" hosts are clueless regarding the presence of a hosting relay. Critical flaws in interconnected objects (mainly IP cameras) were used to deploy the very large DDOS attack campaign that hit the United States in 2016. The sheer power of these campaigns exceeded any previous known DDOS campaigns. Information security firms crafted many hypotheses of attribution, until it became probable that the initial trigger for the DDOS campaign could have been a videogame aficionado "experimenting" with hacking tool suites, and targeting Sony Playstation Network, before it became out of control. This attribution scenario is very unlikely.

The third ambiguity resides in the ubiquity and malleability of the Internet addressing architecture. Most legal attempts to use the ownership of an IP address as an evidence of crime failed to counter-proliferate organized cybercrime. The French HADOPI law incriminates the owner of an IP address for downloading illegal contents. The law has been efficient in supporting police work in enforcing France's regulatory framework, and accessory to the arrest of several child pornography networks in France. But organized cybercrime organizations are very unlikely to use or borrow an IP address without decoy, obfuscation and proper hiding of the original point of emission of the attack campaign. The comparison of cyber attacks with traditional warfare is confronted with an inextricable deadlock: an unaware accomplice can deploy the weapon. Subsequently, can we compare a cyber attack to a the use of armed force under article 2–4 or an "armed attack" under article 51 of the charter of the United Nations?

The question is less trivial that its formulation suggests. It raises not only the question of the neutrality of information technology, but especially its boundaries with private law, commercial law and public law in cyberspace. If we consider computer technology as a neutral element, we must therefore accept the idea that

[34]For instance, Edward Snowden claimed that he did not steal any credentials, did not break any code, and did not temper any security protection when he gathered information from his employer. He used the access that was granted to him.

the establishment of evidence, attribution of aggression, can no longer be resolved by a simple computer audit.

Regulating the cyberspace is similar to buying a passport for interfering in the internal affairs of its neighbors. At least that is how it is perceived in many articles of the Budapest Convention, in particular article 32, which relates to cross-border access to "data", during crises, incidents or investigations. The regulation of the counter-measure, that is to say, the legitimacy to engage in retaliation and to assess its proportionality, is obviously at the heart of the dispute.

The West is pushing a vision of attacks attribution close to common law, which would infer the responsibility for the crimes to their geographical origin; and the "right of retaliate" to a form of extra-territoriality granted by these treaties. But, since their writing, the technologies have changed and the geographical allocation of the modern attack campaigns is almost impossible. Nation-States eventually have their own effective regulatory frameworks against petty cybercrime, when naive or ill-equipped attackers fail to hide the origin of an attack. But modern Nation-States are still unable to frame the advanced and persistent attacks (APTs), led by organized crime, which are capable of avoiding detection and deterrence frameworks.

Some of the partners of these negotiations see it as a "carte blanche" given to the nations that have a technological advantage to conduct a "limited war" or a "dirty war". The problem is that, in terms of crime, the motive and the place of the crime is far from being sufficient to establish intentionality and the identity of the culprit! The modern cyber-war suggests an emergent dominant paradigm of *limited warfare* that resembles counterinsurgency tactics: the means are borrowed, converted, moved, and subversive by nature. The intensive use of robotic capabilities (botnets, etc.) makes it complex to establish an intentional source. The model proposed by current regulation frameworks is closely inspired by conventional conflicts, including, for example, notions such as escalation of the conflict. But who would be the first victims of a cyber-escalation? The first victims would probably be those who most depend on the digital infrastructure, from an economic point of view. The Chinese or the Russians have made different strategic choices in the development of their more vertical national information infrastructures. They developed compartmentalized networks, in part, with proprietary technologies, developed since the mid-1980s; certainly slower, but much less sensitive to an escalation of damages in the event of a conflict.[35]

The problem of regulation remains the *point of access*, that is to say, the anchor point of the digital economy. In the 2007–2017 decade, the United States primarily focused on the importance of intellectual property theft with a loss of 4.8/5 billion, according to a US Congress' report.[36] This eagerness hides a major vulnerability

[35]Even if taking into account the superior redundancy of open networks. For additional reading on cyber-resilience, see: Keys et al. (2016).

[36]cf. *USTR Special 301 Report on Protection of American Intellectual Property Rights Across the World*, Office of the United States Trade Representative, April 2016 https://ustr.gov/sites/de-fault/files/USTR-2016-Special-301-Report.pdf.

from the industry itself. Today, the point of creation of value, the anchor point of business models, and the point of confrontation of cyber-conflict is the same: computer networks.

With e-commerce becoming a dominant form of commercial transactions, formation of opinions directly dependent on human-machine interfaces (Google, Facebook, or MSFT among others). The lever for the creation of national wealth is inseparable from the global cyber battlefield. It probably explains the divergence of agendas between industry majors—who want a model where each citizen is the holder of an operating license of its own personal data—, and sovereign States over intellectual property. Transparency and access required by States are not necessarily in the interest of the industry. This has led some Nation States to refuse to continue this kind of conversation, not by concern for the defense of personal liberties, as they continue to violate them blithely, but in order to prevent the international regulation of cyber defense to disrupt their sovereign interests.

The issue of "counter-measures" poses the question of whether it is the most competent, the sovereign, or the infrastructure manager, who must take up arms and defeat the attacker. The doctrine of "competence" is one of the technologists. It leads, of course, to an enacted extra-territoriality of suppliers, and behind them, an *imperatur* to a "right to audit" from countries that are the hosts or industrial stakeholders. This scenario is often identified as being promoted by the United States, where the supremacy of the American sector of the cyber-security and the State apparatus for the cyber-defense would establish a pattern that entrusts the technology supplier with the responsibility of counter-measures. This doctrine is opposed to the vertical model of sovereignty defended by Russia, China, and in a less extent, France and Germany. The Europeans, however, are trying to form a common front on the regulation of interception, on the protection of personal data. The positions within Europe are of course varied. The Germans have a different perception of the protection of personal data. Painful memories of pre-reunification Germany are still prevalent.

3.3 The French National Strategy for Cybersecurity

3.3.1 An History of Monopoly, Technological Excellence and Fearless Entrepreneurs

The history of France national cyber-security policy and initiatives is tightly intertwined with the evolution of its signal intelligence history. The first initiative creating a national capability for interception and a central cipher and cryptographic department was launched in 1942 after the Allies recaptured North Africa, and was hence created in Algiers. In December 1942, General de Gaulle asked Colonel Jean Joubert de Ouches to set up a decentralized organization capable of intercepting and deciphering enemy communications. By August 1943, the French committee for the national liberation (CFLN) signed a decree giving birth to an inter-ministerial organization called the *Direction Technique du Chiffre* (Cipher Technical Directorate). Hence, the founding culture of French SIGINT is born through a counter-offensive initiative that will shape its future developments and administrative anchoring. The "Cipher Directorate" (*Département du Chiffre*) was hence a subdivision of the French BCRA (*Bureau central de renseignements et d'action*), with very limited analytical capabilities.

France's national informational culture finds its roots in the creation of the national Post, Telegraph and Telephony (PTT) administration in 1879. A State monopoly led the supervision of all land, telegraphic and radio communications until 1998. As a vertical public organization, the administrative body was placed under the direct authority of a Ministry, which name has evolved during the XXth century to reflect various technological evolutions: land transportation, telegraph, telephony, television, telecommunications, and in the early 1990s, the Internet. The final separation between an administration devoted to telecommunications (France Telecom) and one devoted to mail transportation (La Poste) occurred respectively in 1988 and 1991. Until the early 1990s, the French "users" ("customers" was banished as a term of usage) were placing phone calls, dialing in numeric services (the "Minitel" created in 1981), on State-property terminals. Until the early 1990s, the State and its civil servants hence directed the entire pace of technological adoption and evolution. The consequences were twofold: First, advantageously, the French State was able to be a very early adopter on most historical telecommunication technologies. Second, the vertical monopoly prevented the emergence of a dynamic private market, and slowed the emergence of cyberspace in France.

France was one of the first countries to develop the project of a nation-wide telegraph networks during the French Revolution (1790: "le télégraphe Chappe"), a technology invented by a French national, Guillaume Amontos, in the Garden of Luxembourg in Paris, in 1690. France was also a pioneer in installing international regulation frameworks. In 1865, the international convention on telegraphic communications is signed in Paris, and eventually led to the creation of the International Telecommunication Union (ITU) in 1906 (to later become the CCIF, then CCIT, CCIR, then ITU). Other pioneering outcomes include the creation of the precursor of Internet, the Minitel, in 1981, a nation-wide low broadband network (2400 bauds) allowing for on-line banking, gaming, instant messaging at a very low cost (terminals were rented for a dozen of Francs, with a pay-per-minute model). France was also the country, worldwide, to develop a fully operational Fiber-to-the-home (FTTH) network in the city of Biarritz (1500 subscribers) in the early 1980s. The service provided a 64 kbit/s connection, allowing displaying 625 lines television (15 channels) and a video-on-demand service, at a time when the Internet was very far from being even invented. The first subscribers to this commercial FTTH network started to use the service in 1983.

The paradox of French technological advance is that most of its level of maturation was insured by the State. Hence, while being the precursor of many worldwide technologies, such as Instant Messaging (the "line 0" of the Minitel, created by engineers in 1981, was literally a text-messaging system over the air and broadband networks), France has systematically been the latest to turn these innovations into societal transformation. The first problem was the perception of the trade itself: French telecom engineers belonged to an elite, and an actual administrative corpse ("Corpse of telecommunications") that consider his duty to have the highest quality in transporting voice or data over any distance. This credo and mission did not involve contents, which were perceived as belonging to the media sphere. Hence, when the Minitel was introduced, a dynamic private industry took over content with a truly venal bias: the quality of the services was moderate to poor; barriers to entry were numerous; and other State monopolies (trains, energy, etc.) did very little to open the market to new entrants. Even when France Telecom was partially privatized in 1998 (20% of its workforce), the raise of the Internet was perceived as a distant threat at best; and as a "media" phenomenon at most. As the self-imposed core belief was to do as little as possible with "contents", the telecommunication elite was still trying to push a modernized version of the Minitel (in colors!) as its vision of a walled-garden Internet.

When the "Internet revolution" eventually took place, it had been the work of cunning and regulator's harassment by an outsider, Xavier Niel. Niel was one of these early entrepreneurs of the Minitel who launched an erotic messaging system in the early 1990s; eventually diversifying in 1990, by buying the remaining shares of Fermic Multimedia, and renaming it "Iliad".[37] In 1995, he acquired the first Internet Service Provider in France, "Worldnet", and took on a truly Maverick fight against the main incumbent: France Telecom. Invoking predatory prices and abuse of dominant position from the national operator, Niel challenged France Telecom, and won systematically, in the late 1990s: systematically minimizing financial compensation, he demanded a "fair access" to the national network assets (copper lines, then ADSL, then fiber optic, then GSM, etc.). He won every single case he challenged, and was granted access to every single form of access to State-owned infrastructure, allowing the creation of services at a very low cost (the regulator, under a European Union's liberal framework granted the access, not taking into account the Net Value Added or the maintenance cost of the infrastructure, which was considered already fully depreciated). Hence, Xavier Niel was able to offer a triple-play service at a very low price for the customer (€30 per month), including voice, data and Internet access, surfing on a business model that did not have to carry infrastructural depreciation costs.

This cunning strategy had a very positive outcome: France quickly became one the highest Internet penetration in the world (with 83%), with the cheapest triple play plan on the planet (Xavier Niel's triple play includes free worldwide telephony, and is accordingly called "Free"). To the surprise to the elitist Telecommunication Corpse of engineers, this new entrant also praised QoS (quality of service). While maintaining its attractive pricing, Free gradually ramped up its offer, to include FTTH up to 350 Mo/s at the exact same triple-play plan of €35.

[37]Gilles Sengès, *Xavier Niel : L'homme Free*, édition Michel de Maule, 2012.

3.3.2 *The Directorate of Information System Security (SCSSI, DCSSI) 1986–2009*

The central service for information system security is a former department of the Prime minister, who was part of the general Secretariat of national defense. In 1986, France defined a comprehensive policy for the security of information systems, with the adoption of a series of regulatory texts establishing an interministerial commission and delegation, as well as a central service for the security of information systems. This organization was revised with the assignment in 1996 to the General Secretariat for National Defense (SGDN) of a special responsibility in the identification and monitoring of risks affecting the security of information systems. A central direction for the security of information services (DCSSI), an integral part of the SGDN, was created by a decree of July 31, 2001.

3.3.3 *The Lasbordes (2006) and Romani Reports (2008)*

In a report published on January 13, 2006, entitled, "The security of information systems—A major issue for France",[38] Pierre Lasbordes believed that "France is lagging behind concern in the face of the imperatives of security of information systems, both at the State level than at the level of companies, a few large groups set apart", with such an organization marked by the dispersion and the autonomy of the different actors within the State services, inadequate facilities and businesses vulnerabilities.

One of the main weaknesses highlighted by the Lasbordes report was the conduct of the information systems security policy, which suffered from a wide dispersion of actors and the insufficient authority of the structures responsible for implementing it artwork. The Senator Lasbordes was very severe with the centralized information security organization that he audited in 2005, stating: "The multiplication of public actors, whose missions overlap and whose founding texts are not very precise, gives a general impression of confusion and scattering of means and men. In this nebula, the dedicated public actor, the SGDN and more precisely the DCSSI, suffers from a lack of authority and sometimes credibility with the publics concerned. These two factors, the scattering of resources and the lack of authority of the SGDN, undermine the effectiveness of the State in the definition and implementation of the global information systems security policy".[39]

---

[38] http://www.senat.fr/rap/r11-681/r11-68117.html.

[39] «La multiplication des acteurs publics, dont les missions se chevauchent et dont les textes fondateurs sont peu précis, donne une impression générale de confusion et d'éparpillement des moyens et des hommes. Dans cette nébuleuse, l'acteur public dédié, le SGDN et plus précisément la DCSSI, souffre d'un manque d'autorité et parfois de crédibilité auprès des publics concernés. Ces deux facteurs, l'éparpillement des moyens et le manque d'autorité du SGDN, nuisent à l'efficacité de l'Etat dans la définition et la mise en œuvre de la politique globale de sécurité des systèmes d'information» (extract of the Lasbordes Report, 2006).

One of the elements that struck Senator Lasbordes was the evident lack of resources that were deployed by the French government for its cyberdefense: in total, less than 100 specialized computer security experts worked at the DCSSI. Training was poor, most competencies were lagging of one or two generations, administrations were not sufficiently protected and there was a dramatic lack of understanding of the impact of digitalization on both the craft of governing and defense doctrines. Senator Lasbordes considered that, in general, French companies have insufficiently taken into account the reality of the threat and had not put themselves in a position to protect themselves, except for a few large groups.

In February 2008, the Senate's Committee on Foreign Affairs, Defense and Armed Forces, chaired at the time by Mr Josselin de Rohan, wished to take an interest in this matter and entrusted one of its members, Mr. Roger Romani, to prepare a report on cyber defense. Published on July 8, 2008, the report entitled "Cyber defense: a new national security issue" estimated that France was neither prepared nor organized to deter computer attacks. According to this report, the lack of resources, especially in comparison with British or German neighbors, was undermining the role of a central authority truly capable of driving and coordinating a comprehensive information security policy.

3.3.4 The National Defense White Paper of 2008

The 2008 White Paper on Defense and National Security marked a "turning point" in terms of cyberdefense. Indeed, with the White Paper, the protection of information systems is clearly defined as an integral component of the French national defense and security policy. Remarkably, instead of pursuing a specialization strategy, the report strongly recommended that every aspect of administrative life, military and defense organization and doctrines, would be reformed and re-designed in order to fully integrate digital transformation of defense. The White Paper advocates "the transition from a passive defense strategy to an active defense strategy in depth, combining intrinsic protection of systems, permanent surveillance, rapid reaction and offensive action", such a development assuming "a strong governmental impulse and a change of mentalities".

The White Paper, for the first time, gives an important place to the threat posed by computer attacks. It considered that "the current daily level of attacks on information systems, whether of state or non-state origin, suggests a very high potential for destabilization of everyday life, paralysis of networks critical for the Life of the nation, or the denial of functioning of certain military capabilities". One the core conclusions of the White Paper are that a passive defense would be rarely efficient against cyber-attacks based on advanced information technologies.

3.3.5 The Creation of ANSSI (2009)

The *Agence nationale de la sécurité des systèmes d'information* (ANSSI) is a French service created by decree on 7 July 2009. This service with a national remit is attached to the Secretary general of defense and national security (SGDSN), the authority to assist the Prime minister in the exercise of its responsibilities in the areas of defense and national security. ANSSI replaces the central Management of the security of information systems, created by the decree of 31 July 2001 (art. 10 of the decree of July 7, 2009). Guillaume Poupard, a graduate from Ecole Polytechnique, engineer-in-chief of the armament, was appointed director general of ANSSI march 27, 2014, succeeding Patrick Pailloux.

Its budget amounts to 83,4 million Euros in 2014 and its staff to 350 people, with a target of 500 agents end 2015 and 567 the end of 2017. By way of comparison, the counterparts to the ANSSI in Germany and the United Kingdom have between 500 and 700 people.

These organizations, initially created in a military perspective of information security and protection, have gradually evolved. By 1986, the central service for cryptography and security of telecommunications (*Service central du chiffre et de la sécurité des telecommunications*) had been replaced by the central service for information system security. In 2017, ANSSI pursues a mission of information systems security for the State, but it is also in charge of a mission to provide advice and support to administrations and operators of vital importance (OIV).

3.3.6 The 2010 Cybersecurity Group of the High Council for Strategic Education and Research (CSFRS)

In 2010, the French Presidency created a national security strategic council, aiming at gathering a broad range of expertise, civilian and military, industrial and governmental, scientific and academic, to conduct a "strategizing" function for France Prime Minister. Labeled "High Council for Strategic Education and Research" (CSFRS), the Scientific Council included "Contemporary Threats And Information Technologies, New Criminalities".[40] Led by Jean-Marc Suchier, the group produced an executive synthesis on France cyberdefense and cybersecurity organization in 2011 that became instrumental in further policy changes. The group concluded that "the penetration which affected French organizations showed without ambiguity that the systems of sensitization, of awareness, of understanding

[40]Chairman of the Working Group: Jean-Marc Suchier. Members: Cédric Blancher (deceased), Airbus; Jean-Louis Bruguière; Yves Deswarte (deceased), LAAS-CNRS; Jean-Michel Duccoroy, Ministry of the Interior; David Hotte, BPCE; F. Bernard Huyghe, Univ. Paris IV; Sophie de Lastours, Historian, ARCSI; Hélène Martini, Ecole des commissaires de police; Stanislas de Maupeou, THALES; Ludovic Mé, Supélec; Jean-Pierre Pochon, Honorary Dir. of Nat. Pol.

risks and of regulation and control are today neither efficient, nor understood or applied" (op. cit., p. 46). The report also stressed that the "French legal framework is too much restrictive, as illustrated by the ban on reverse analysis for security reasons. In addition, it is almost impossible to deal in a proper and reasonable manner with the discovery and publication of new vulnerabilities or new attack methods" (op. cit., p. 48)

The Group's conclusion embraced Cybersecurity as a "power equalizer" in the twenty-first century. As the national report stated: "The realization of the value of assets to be protected and the true extent of the threats to be evaluated are always the result of a successful attack. Recent examples of penetration which affected French organizations showed without ambiguity that the systems of sensitization, of awareness, of understanding risks and of regulation and control are today neither efficient, nor understood or applied.[41] The report stressed the importance of securing the raising digitalization of the French society, suggesting that digital sovereignty is weakened by imported and homogenous protocols; the lack of national norms and enforcement; the poor exploitation of the French national expertise, private and public, in cyberdefense and Cybersecurity.

The report called for the creation of a national observatory, including a national network of CERTs, at the operational level; and a public-private coordination body, "whose mission will be to verify the implementation of security recommendations, to assess the cyber security level of society, to report major incidents, to give recommendations to public and private operators, and to make public the test results concerning the most critical systems" (ibid.). The proposed national plan for cyber strategy would have included "Create a national methodology for the evaluation of the security of information systems based on an internationally recognized standard. Design a process of national certification involving the French regulatory organization ANSSI (National Agency for the Security of Information Systems) and approved certification organizations" (ibid., p. 48).

The report stressed the importance of attracting world-class skills in the field of Cybersecurity. Noticeably, the Group recommended a "relaxation of regulatory constraints", in order to foster advanced R&D in cyberdefense. The national regulation prevented laboratory attack campaigns, as the act of conducting a computerized attack were already sanctioned in the French law. Unambiguously, the report stated: "The regulatory framework of research and publication of new vulnerabilities must be defined to avoid the present ambiguities and obstacles: Obstacles to innovation and research, with associated accelerated brain drain" (ibid.).

Being a hybrid organization between a national think-tank and a strategy formulation body for the State, the CSFRS report had decisive influence on the national cyberdefense reform thinking. Many of its recommendations called for a reinforcement of ANSSI,[42] both in terms of capabilities and in the role of an

[41]*CSFRS National Strategy Report*, Paris: CNRS Editions, 2012.

[42]National Agency for the Security of Information Systems.

expertise platform (pentest, certifications, norms, independent body of expertise). The report also stressed the vital role of a dynamic SME industry in the field of Cybersecurity, stressing that it would be "an illusion to believe that France will achieve convincing results if human resources do not live up to ambitions in respect of both research and industrialization" (ibid., p. 49).

Interestingly, the Group's report underlined the importance of "offensive competencies", judging these capabilities "inexistent" in 2010 (p. 49): "The offensive competencies of France seem to us of course very much inferior to those of the United States of America, but also to those of England or Germany. There is here an important challenge to be taken up".

3.3.7 The 2011 National Digital Strategy

The resulting digital societal culture of this troubling history is a founding stone of France's national digital strategy. As the State monopoly missed out its strategic turn to tackle the Internet, the situation was one of high distress. The cyberspace became the arena were opinions were forged, polls were changed, and the State had lost touch with the digital media. In 2011, the French government decided to put together a "national strategy" aiming at repositioning the State and its sovereign interests at the center of the national development of the French cyberspace. On April 29, 2011, the French government created the Digital National Council[43] (*Conseil national du numérique*[44]), an independent consultative body of 30 members, with the objective of reinstating the role of the State in fostering growth in the digital area, protecting a domestic Net neutrality, and defending freedom of expression and privacy of data on the "French Internet". One year later, the whole council offered its resignation, and was swiftly replaced by a new, and more compliant, team led by Jean-Baptiste Soufron. The first national report is published in November 2011, and is entitled "France Numérique 2012–2020"[45].

The least that can be said about this first national strategy is that it was belated, and it did not address any decisive strategic issue. After a self-glorifying introduction about national achievements, including the best European 4G network (along with Sweden, Germany and the United States), the report praised the cheap Triple Play offers (at 35 Euros), forgetting to mention the decisive role played by Mr. Xavier Niel and its "Free" ISP. Most recommendations were focused on leveraging national broadband access; supporting the development of a content

[43]http://cnnumerique.fr/missions/.

[44]https://www.legifrance.gouv.fr/affichTexte.do?cidTexte=JORFTEXT000023928752&-dateTexte=&categorieLien=id.

[45]http://archives.entreprises.gouv.fr/2012/www.industrie.gouv.fr/tic/france-numerique2020/2011_plan_france_numerique2020.pdf.

industry; improving the "governance" of the digital society (a battle already long lost at the national level).

By the year 2012, the initial report found pragmatic applications in leveraging European Union federal funds to support the development of Internet start-ups, and to increase the Internet penetration in rural areas. France, however, is not an exception, and most of its "white zones" (geographical zones with poor or absent connectivity) are not addressable with a sound economic model. While the plan achieved success in urban areas, the pace of adoption among SMEs in rural areas did not really take off. Despite an investment of €2 billion for a nation-wide enhanced Internet infrastructure, the determinant variable of France's national digital growth remained the price war led by Xavier Niel's Free. On the other hand, the €2.25 billion invested in the support of the emergence of digital start-ups did bring satisfying results; with a steep increase in start-up creation in Paris, Lyon and Toulouse.

3.3.8 The 2012 Bockel Report on Cyberdefense

In 2011 and early 2012, several large scale attack campaigns struck French national interests, which motivated the Senate's *Committee on foreign affairs, defense and armed forces* to launch a special inquiry into the French cyberdefense's organization and eventual weaknesses. The first of these attacks was conducted on the French Presidency information systems, and on the Ministry of Finance headquarters while France was presiding the G20. A second series of attacks were directed to Areva, the French national champion in nuclear energy. The Bockel report noticeably stated, "Other States may carry out these cyber attacks by computer hackers, activist groups, criminal organizations, as well as by competitor companies". The report encouraged that more budget shall be attributed to the national agency for information system security (ANSSI), noting "With a staff of 230 people and a budget of 75 million Euros, ANSSI still lags far behind similar departments in the United Kingdom or Germany, which have between 500 and 700 agents".[46]

3.3.9 The 2016 French National Digital Security Strategy

Under the leadership of Manuel Valls, then Prime Minister of France, a complete renewal of the French national cybersecurity strategy was undertaken in 2016. The government engaged into a large consultation with many stakeholders, including large IT corporations, banks, cybersecurity consultancies, personnel of the Ministry

[46]Bockel Report, 2012.

of Interior, Defense and Foreign Affairs. Several subtle but decisive changes were made in the conceptual framework of this new strategy.

The terminology evolved. "Sovereign interests" were replaced with "fundamental interests" in a more ambiguous but also more flexible elaboration that includes critical infrastructures, strategic industries (nuclear, energy, water, gas, transportation, etc.). The explicit objective is to differentiate the French national strategy both from a technologist perspective (identified by French policy-makers as being carried out by the United States) and from the vertical and sovereign doctrines espoused by China and Russia. Instead of promoting territoriality, the new doctrine promotes the "defense of its fundamental interests in cyberspace".

The renewed national strategy does not separate the defense of national interests from the fight against cybercrime. This doctrine corroborates a shift in national defense policy that took place with the 2008 national defense white paper. Security is seen as a *continuum* from the protection of the people (police, interior, civil liberties, infrastructures) to the defense of its military and strategic prerogatives. "Cyber malevolence" is identified as a broad target for a passive and dynamic defense, which includes both passive monitoring and active retaliation when "France national interests are at stake".

This critical shift in the design and purpose of the French national cybersecurity was motivated by the terrorist attacks against the French population in the years 2015–2016. The government proposed to "renovate" the French legal framework for intelligence gathering, by enlarging its prerogative to digital media, computer networks, and hence, absorbing all the constituents of the cyber domain. The new "Law for Intelligence" (*Loi relative au renseignement)* encountered a vivid opposition from activist groups and from parliamentary members. The law received more than 434 amendments in the first months of the Assembly debate. The Senate then iterated 227 new amendments in between May and June 2015.[47] Facing resistance, the French President decided to inquire the Constitutional council. The move was interpreted as singular as the recourse to the Constitutional council is usually engaged when a law is contrary to the European legal framework. Within a month, 60 French deputies decided to also challenge the law with the Constitutional council.

A wide opposition arose to the text, which proposed a real time interception of every French digital communications, including IP connections, e-mails, telephony, voice-over-ip and instant messaging. The law was inspired by the US Patriot Act, enacting the capability for French intelligence services to gather continuously and in real time the meta-data (origin, destination, length, etc.) of every communications originating or transiting through the French territory. The Law indicated that the intelligence services would use several algorithms; however, their cryptographic method and keys would be published in a secret executive order; in other words, not accessible to the public. The main objective of the Law was to gain a strategic

---

[47]Initial project of the Law on April 16, 2015: http://www.assemblee-nationale.fr/14/ta-pdf/2697-p.pdf.

advantage in the cyber-war against the Islamic State. But experts were swift to point out that most of the contents distributed by the Islamic State were broadcasted on encrypted networks, did not originate from the French territory, and that the final distribution (Youtube, Dailymotion, etc.) was itself broadcast using standard encryption (HTTPS).

The most virulent opponents of the Law were the institutions that the French government had created to promote personal privacy and freedom of information in France. The French National commission for computing and freedom (CNIL), the National Digital Council (*Conseil national du numérique*) called the project an Orwellian "mass surveillance". The French magistrate union (*Syndicat de la magistrature*) heavily criticized a project that "dispossessed" the judge in order to give executive powers a full control over personal data, privacy and freedom of expression. On May 31, 2015, the New York Times published an editorial entitled "The French Surveillance State".[48]

The Law is finally enacted,[49] the same year on July 24, 2015, and modified[50] on July 21, 2016; benefiting from the recently enacted "State of emergency". Although considered as an anti-terrorist law, the "*Loi relative au renseignement*" is truly an advanced legal cyber-deterrence framework. In its article L. 822-2, the law states: "In the strict and necessary measure required by technical analysis, and excluding its utilization for the surveillance of the concerned individuals, collected intelligence that contains encrypted data, and the decrypted intelligence gathered from this data, can be stored beyond the legal time of the present law".[51] In other words, when an intelligence operation is conducted to deter a cyber attack, every data can be stored and kept indefinitely. The initial Law was reinforced by several executive orders, a means to escape the attention of the Press. An executive order from January 31, 2016 literally allowed the French intelligence services to use any existing technical means to conduct cyber operations: geographical location of terminals, networks, on-line communications, connection data, and software access.[52]

The 2016 National Digital Strategy also strongly reinforced the security of information systems of "operators of vital importance". This legal framework was

[48]https://www.nytimes.com/2015/04/01/opinion/the-french-surveillance-state.html?_r=0 In its article L. 821-7, magistrates, members of the parliament, lawyers and journalists are excluded from the scope of the Law.

[49]https://www.legifrance.gouv.fr/affichTexte.do?cidTexte=JORFTEXT000030931899-&fastPos=1&fastReqId=1051131699&categorieLien=id&oldAction=rechTexte.

[50]https://www.legifrance.gouv.fr/affichTexte.do?cidTexte=JORFTEXT000032921910&fastPos-=1&fastReqId=1562450731&categorieLien=id&oldAction=rechTexte.

[51]"*Dans une mesure strictement nécessaire aux besoins de l'analyse technique et à l'exclusion de toute utilisation pour la surveillance des personnes concernées, les renseignements collectés qui contiennent des éléments de cyberattaque ou qui sont chiffrés, ainsi que les renseignements déchiffrés associés à ces derniers, peuvent être conservés au-delà des durées mentionnées au présent I*".

[52]https://www.legifrance.gouv.fr/affichTexte.do?cidTexte=JORFTEXT000031940885&-dateTexte=&categorieLien=id.

designed within the 2013 national defense white paper, and then enacted into the Articles 21 and 22 of the Law n° 2013-1168. This strategy is not only normative. The French defense supports the innovative creations of French young cybersecurity start-ups, actively seeking to gain technological breakthroughs in emerging fields (deep learning, AI, autonomous systems). It also actively surveys the open source community for disruptive technologies in hardware (USB key testers), firmware, embedded security. The national agency ANSSI is actively seeking new volunteers for its certification program, but this program is mainly outsourced to information security firms. A low-level certification audit cost nearly 60 K€ in 2016, which is way above the cost of similar product certifications in the United States, England or Germany. These important barriers to mobility, and prohibitive costs, have deterred many high-performing French cybersecurity start-ups that simply left France to reinstall their activities abroad. The grand total of these "certified suppliers" were less than 25 in January 2017.[53] Most of these certified cybersecurity providers are large French incumbents: Cassidian Cybersecurity (now Airbus Defense and Space), Bull, CGI, CS, Ernst and Young, Steria, Orange, PWCA, Sogeti and Thales. Young, R&D intensive, innovative cybersecurity start-ups are clearly outnumbered, that led many observers to assume that logic of club was superseding the certification logic.[54]

This situation was tackled by the 2016 national digital strategy, and a tremendous effort has been deployed by ANSSI to certify more SMEs and more innovative start-ups. Innovative SMEs still represent less than 10% of certified suppliers in early 2017.

France has also decided in its 2016 national strategy to align with NATO and the EU: "It is up to the CERT-EU (Computer Emergency Response Team of the European Union (EU) institutions, bodies and agencies) and to the NCIRC (Computer Incidence Response Capability) within the North Atlantic Treaty Organization (NATO) to ensure the cyberdefense of their respective institutions".[55] However, this early strategic alignment was swiftly put aside in the declarations of the Minister of Defense concerning France national military cyberdefense strategies on December 12, 2016.

Interestingly, France belongs to a very small group of nations, in our comparative study of national doctrines, which *acknowledges* the necessity of rejuvenating traditional strategic doctrines to adapt them to cyber. Existing assessments of

---

[53]For a complete list: https://www.ssi.gouv.fr/administration/qualifications/prestataires-de-services-de-confiance-qualifies/prestataires-daudit-de-la-securite-des-systemes-dinformation-passi-qualifies/.

[54]For more on "Club Theory", see: Sandler and Tschirhart (1997).

[55]*National Digital Strategy Report*, 2016, Publication of the French Government, Unclassified—Public, p. 17.

France cyber readiness level have utterly missed this point.[56] As the 2016 National digital strategy points out: "Although digital technology fundamentally changes our societies, its impact on other realities such as those of sovereignty, national territory, currency or the fundamental interests of the Nation is yet to be measured and the organization and means of public action to make the law apply to it or to ensure their protection must be reconsidered. A discussion, coordinated by the General Secretary of Defense and National Security, will be held to develop an intellectual corpus related to cyberspace." (ibid., p. 17).

This point is even more prevalent in the inclusion of a cultural defense policy within the cybersecurity framework: "Digital platforms, including social networks, can shape opinion more insidiously and are often vectors of values that are not those of the French Republic" (op cit, p. 17). Propaganda, disinformation, cyber-destabilization and manipulation of information in the objective to threaten France national interests were included in the category of "fundamental interests". The report states (ibid.) that they belong to a category of "are attack on defense and national security which is sanctioned by law."

The 2016 National digital strategy, in many aspects, sounded like a warning for friends and foes. France would not allow large international corporations and foreign states spying on its people. In the sophisticated language that characterizes French national reports: "Digital technology development cannot be sustainable in a cyberspace where States do not respect the good practices required for a balanced digital transition that is beneficial to all nations and where a few economic players monopolize the wealth that constitutes digital data, notably personal data, true resources for future generations."

This integration of French republican values (*laïcité*, fundamental right of expression) into a national cyber strategy framework constitutes an in-depth strategic shift with the previous doctrines.[57]

---

[56]In particular, the M. Hattaway, C. Demchak, J. Kerben, J. McArdle and F. Spidalieri's report, "France Cyber Readiness at a Glance", September 2016, *Potomac Institute for Policy Studies*. The report suffered from a lack of access to reliable and high ranked sources. However, lowering external perceptions has always been at the core of French national strategic policies, which are grounded into a cultural benevolence towards ill-informed publications.

[57]We accordingly positioned in our comparative study of national doctrines both editions of France national cybersecurity strategies from 2008 (*initial Livre Blanc de la Défense*) and 2016 (*Stratégie digitale nationale*). As we will later see, in next Sect. 4.1, the French national doctrine shifted from a very defensive and technocratic defensive doctrine, to a more societal, dynamic and offensive cyber-doctrine.

References

Alperovitch D (2016) Bears in the midst: intrusion into the democratic national committee. Crowdstrike Blog post, 15 June 2016. https://www.crowdstrike.com/blog/bears-midst-intrusion-democratic-national-committee/

Bart J, Pieters W (2009) Electronic voting in the Netherlands: from early adoption to early abolishment. In: Foundations of security analysis and design V. Lecture notes in computer science, vol 5705, pp 121–144

Baumard P (1994) From information warfare to knowledge warfare: preparing for the paradigm shift. In: Schwartau W (ed) Information warfare. Thunder's Mouth Press, New York, pp 611–626

Baumard P (2010) Information crises and crisis information. In: Bates MJ, Maack N (eds) Encyclopedia of library and information sciences, 3rd edn, pp 2409–2414

Fallière N, Lima O, Murchu et Eric Chien (2011) W32.Stuxnet Dossier, Symantec. http://www.h4ckr.us/library/Documents/ICS_Events/Stuxnet%20Dossier%20(Symantec)%20v1.4.pdf

Farwell JP, Rohozinski R (2011) Stuxnet and the future of cyber war. Survival Glob Polit Strategy 53(1):23–40

Fleck D (2012) Searching for international rules applicable to cyber warfare—a critical first assessment of the New Tallinn manual. Int J Conflict Secur Law 18(2):331–351

Franceschi-Bicchierai L (2015) Meet Babar, a New Malware almost certainly created by France. Motherboard, 18 Feb 2015. http://motherboard.vice.com/read/meet-babar-a-new-malware-almost-certainly-created-by-france

Kenneth G (2010) The challenge of cyber attack deterrence. Comput Law Secur Rev 26(3):298–303

Keys B, Chhajer A, Liu Z, Horner D (2016) A framework for assessing cyber resilience. World Economic Forum, April 2016. http://bloustein.rutgers.edu/wp-content/uploads/2016/05/2016_WEF.pdf

Kushner D (2013) The real story of stuxnet. IEEE Spectr 50(3):48–53

Lindsay JR (2013) Stuxnet and the limits of cyber warfare. Secur Stud 22(3):365–404

Maunder M (2016) US Govt data shows Russia used outdated Ukrainian PHP Malware. WordFence Blogpost, 30 Dec 2016. https://www.wordfence.com/blog/2016/12/russia-malware-ip-hack/

Michel VE, Nieuwenhuijs A, Luiijf E, Klaver M, Cruz E (2011) The state and the threat of cascading failure across critical infrastructures: the implications of empirical evidence from media incident reports. Public Adm 89(2):381–400

Sandler T, Tschirhart J (1997) Club theory: thirty years later. Public Choice 93(3/4):335–355

Schmitt MN (ed) (2013) The Tallinn manual on the international law applicable to cyber warfare. NATO Cooperative Cyber Defence Centre of Excellence et Cambridge University Press, Tallinn, Estonia

Schmitt MN (2014) The law of cyber warfare: quo vadis? Stanford Law Policy Rev 269:275

Sun L, Hong B, Hacquebord F (2015) Pawn storm update: iOS espionage app found. TrendLabs Security Intelligence Blog, 4 Feb 2015. http://blog.trendmicro.com/trendlabs-security-intelligence/pawn-storm-update-ios-espionage-app-found/?linkId=12146208

Talbot Jensen E (2010) Cyber warfare and precautions against the effects of attacks. Texas Law Rev 88:1533–1570

Chapter 4
National Cyber-Doctrines: Forthcoming Strategic Shifts

Abstract This chapter presents a comparison and positioning of several national cyber-doctrines, and an overview of the technological changes that are shaping national policies and national defense systems. In particular, the chapter questions radical changes in technology that are lagging in both comprehension and implementation into cyber-doctrines and national cyber-defense systems.

Keywords Intrusion detection systems · Machine learning · Non supervised learning · Anomaly detection · Superiority of autonomous defense

4.1 Comparing National Cyber-Doctrines

The technology used in these large-scale campaigns does not dramatically differ from the early days of hacking. 125 lines of codes are still very efficient in 2013 to conduct the exploitation of vulnerabilities, even when the lines of defense have exponentially grown in the past 25 years. As most innovation disruptions in the early twenty-first century, the performance of these campaigns is rooted in the accessibility and diffusion of combinatory learning, i.e. the capacity of outpacing the defensive learning of targets by a better and faster behavioral intelligence.

The formation of two distinctive groups (large-scale spontaneous groups vs. sponsored targeted large scale campaigns) is typical of the two paths that can be used to attain a superior collective behavioral learning advantage. Large spontaneous groups benefit from distributed astute learning, i.e. the learning conducted by individual hackers who can coordinate on a very large scale, making their collective learning ubiquitous and efficient. Targeted sponsored campaigns (such as APTs) benefit from the advance of automated artificial intelligence embedded into technology (e.g. Stuxnet, FLAME).

Most defensive systems are based on the recognition of signatures ("embedded malicious codes") of malwares, or on the normative analysis of behaviors compared to "healthy behaviors" (knowledge-based detection systems). Both the collective learning of spontaneous groups, and advanced machine learning currently outpace

P. Baumard, *Cybersecurity in France*, SpringerBriefs in Cybersecurity,
DOI 10.1007/978-3-319-54308-6_4

signature-based detection systems. The nature of the current paradigm shift is, in this sense, very similar to the evolution of information warfare in the early 1990s. We are witnessing a strategic disruption where defenders are consolidating their information infrastructures, while attackers are engaging in knowledge-warfare.[1] Superior knowledge, through astute combination, can be gained from truncated and partial information. Superior information may not defeat even poorly articulated knowledge.

A *behavioral intelligence paradigm* is synonym with an inescapable rise of "zero days" threats. Pervasive and highly available combinatory learning allows the creation of many variants of an exploit (exploitation of a vulnerability) within 24 h of its discovery. Re-encapsulating and re-combining exploits of undiscovered flaws ("zero days") is made possible by the advancement of causative learning techniques, or when inaccessible, by the very large number of spontaneous hacking groups sharing their recombination experiments. In such a paradigm, focusing on ex-post defense strategy based on known and identified vulnerabilities is likely to fail.

Gathering data from public sources on published Cyber-Defense doctrines, we try in the second part of this analysis to assess the soundness of Cyber-Doctrines for the deterrence of behavioral intelligence-driven threats. We analyzed 35 national strategies to fight cyber-crime, implement cyber-defense, and promote resilient information infrastructures and cyber-security (Fig. 4.1).

We used the framework developed earlier on the history of cyber-criminality to categorize four categories of Cyber-Crimes, based on their destination ("targeted and long-reach" vs. "immediate or non-directed") and their preparation ("spontaneous" vs. "prepared and sponsored"). Hence, we identify four classes of cyber-crime: "code warriors" (I), "cyber free riders" (II), "autonomous collectives" (III) and "sponsored attackers" (IV).

Different classes of attacks require different responses. Immediate and spontaneous attacks (Class I) can be handled with robust information security, including causative learning that can deter sophisticated AI attacks. Most national doctrines have a sound understanding and appropriate range of responses for such attacks. Prepared and sponsored immediate attacks (computer theft by organize crime, free-riding, phishing and cracking—Class II) require a coordinated range of technical and jurisdictional responses. Signature-based detection systems and knowledge-based defenses are usually sufficient to deter most threats, as far as regulation is judicially enforced. Socially and society-rooted attacks (hactivist groups, temporary of goal-driven groups with political, societal or economic motives—Class III) involves perception warfare, information warfare, sense-making capabilities as to respond to rapid and emergent distributed deployment. Finally, offensive campaigns with embedded behavioral intelligence (Class IV) require transversal responses that encompass proactive deterrence "beyond tech" and "beyond claim". Class III and Class IV threats call for real-time

[1]Baumard (1994).

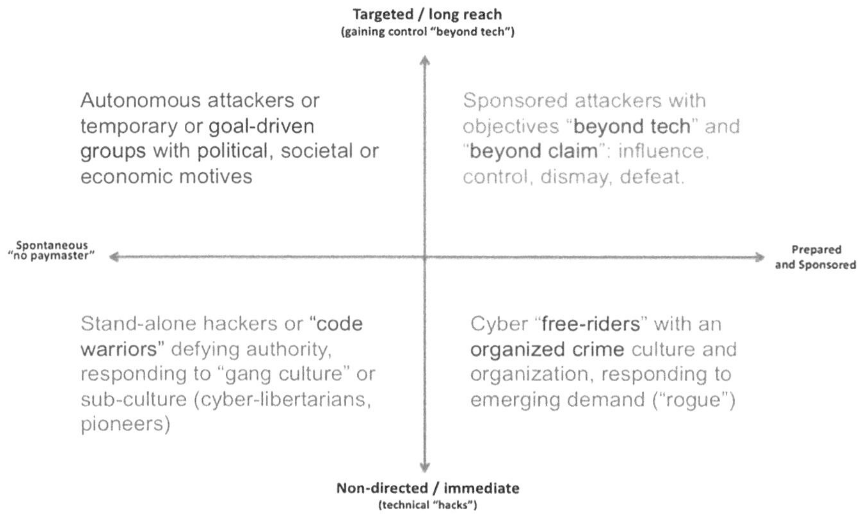

Fig. 4.1 Classification of cyber-attacks

sense-making on unprecedented scales, involving large-scale human cognitive learning on one side (III) and large-scale behavioral learning on the other side (IV).

Our analysis of the evolution of national cyber-crime doctrines over the period 1994–2017 brings mixed findings. "*Power-sovereign*" *doctrines* (P-S, Class IV) emphasize the development of large specialized units, are often obsessed with critical infrastructures protection, and develop more or less publicly, offensive capabilities. While they deliver sustainable deterrence policies on State-sponsored cyber attacks, they usually develop a threat-rigidity dominant logic, which impedes their involvement in emergent societal change.

The risk for P-S doctrines is therefore disconnecting with emergent hacking movements, and a lack of reactivity to distributed cognitive warfare. "*Societal Resilience*" doctrines (Class III), on the other hand, are more sensitive to opinion movements, try to leverage the public space, and focus their offensive capabilities on information warfare. Motivation for such doctrines is not always rooted in a democratic and progressive view of the Internet. Yet, the digitalization of society is clearly identified as both the core threat and core opportunity for cyber-defense and cyber-development. Finally, "Social order" doctrines (Class I) and "Technocratic" doctrines (Class II) only differ in their perception of control. The main difference lies in a control at the source (I) versus a control by a normalization of the outputs (II).

Technocratic perspectives often suffer from a delayed perception of technological change, mainly inspired by an incident-response philosophy or a late entry to the field. Doctrines that favor social order generally suffer from a lack of national vision or national strategy, or have built their policies by borrowing (or aligning to) external national visions (Fig. 4.2).

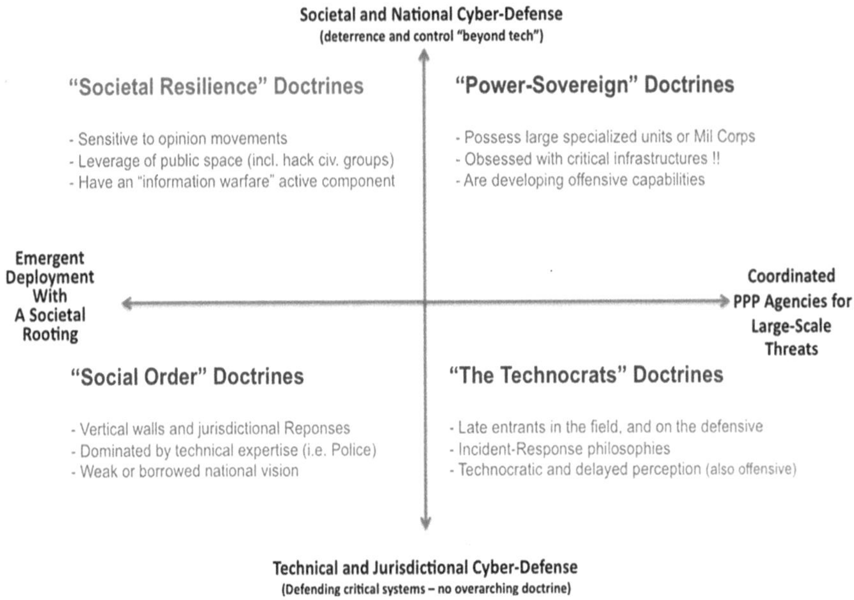

Fig. 4.2 A typology of national cyber-doctrines

4.1.1 *Comparing National Strategies*

Most of the studied national strategies derive their national cyber criminality deterrence with an average delay of 10–15 years with the advancement of technology. Accordingly, society-wide disruptions have been systematically overlooked. Typically, cyber-policies grow in the fourth class, while the most disruptive change is taking place in the third.

Core hacking technologies have been steadily stable in the 1990–2012 period. Advanced Persistent Threats (APTs) are not per se the result of a disruption in core exploits, but rather a paradigmatic change coming from peripheral technologies (mainly: machine learning, automation, combinatory reconfiguration). Such a paradigmatic change thrives on the obsolescence of an aging infrastructure. Combinations are made possible when flaws can be exploited cross-systems. The growing interoperability of vulnerable systems increases the probability of the on-the-fly exploitation of cross-vulnerabilities. In such a context, vendors, by pushing cyber-criminality deterrence to focus on "points of access" vulnerability assessment impedes the investment in behavioral learning technologies (by maintaining a poorly performing, but highly profitable, signature-based defense paradigm).

The following graph presents the positioning of different national cyber-crime deterrence and cyber-defense strategies (year indicates date of first document analyzed). Findings illustrate the trade-off between national policies that focused on organized cyber-crime and policies driven by the surveillance (or the support) of the societal rooting of cyber-developments (Fig 4.3).

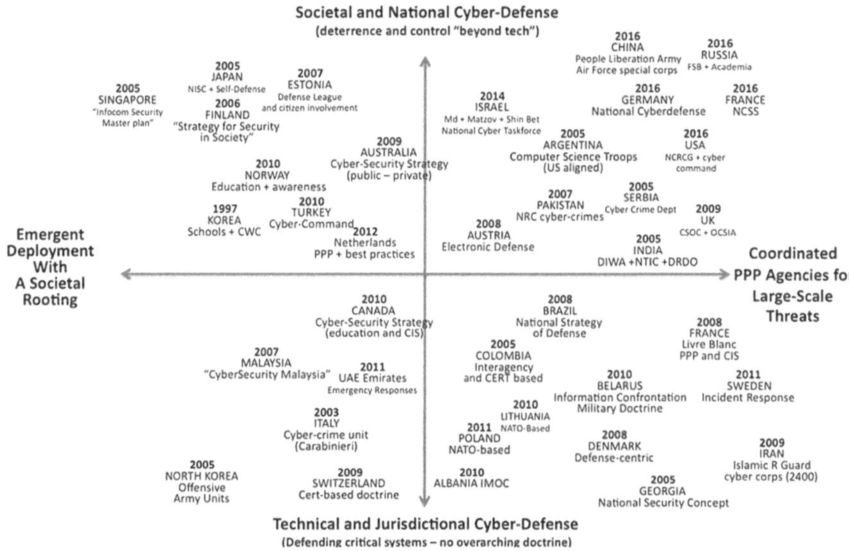

Fig. 4.3 Positioning national doctrines

The only way to counter-act and deter intelligent behaviors is by outpacing and outsmarting its behavioral intelligence. Very few studied doctrines have acknowledged this core systemic vulnerability. Confidence building and security measures (CBSMs) are hence rooted in a technological and societal understanding that may foster vulnerabilities, and suffer from a critical blind spot on the nature of future technological threats.

Technocratic (Class II) and social order (Class I) national doctrines are dependent on vertical and jurisdictional knowledge, while the evolution of threats is horizontal and a-jurisdictional. Most recent large-scale campaigns (APT1, Blaster-worm, etc.) have shown the limits of inter-jurisdictional coordination in responding to attacks with unpredictable attribution, unknown or undiscovered signatures, and using causative learning to adapt to common technical responses (Fig. 4.4).

Most of the analyzed doctrines presented an outdated perception of authorship and attribution. Attribution is assimilated in most doctrines with a geographical point of emission (or several), a central intent, and a legalist perspective on tracking back attacks. Erasing traces of presence, or traces of intrusion, has been long mastered by the hacking community, leading to the conclusion that diplomatic efforts are geared towards resolving an issue that has lost its technological pertinence since 2007.

Understanding the social psychology of threats development is becoming critical, as we are entering a pioneering period that strangely resembles of the "phreaking" years of hacking (1972–1987). The improved portability of machine learning (embarked, distributed or fully autonomous) is curiously absent from most

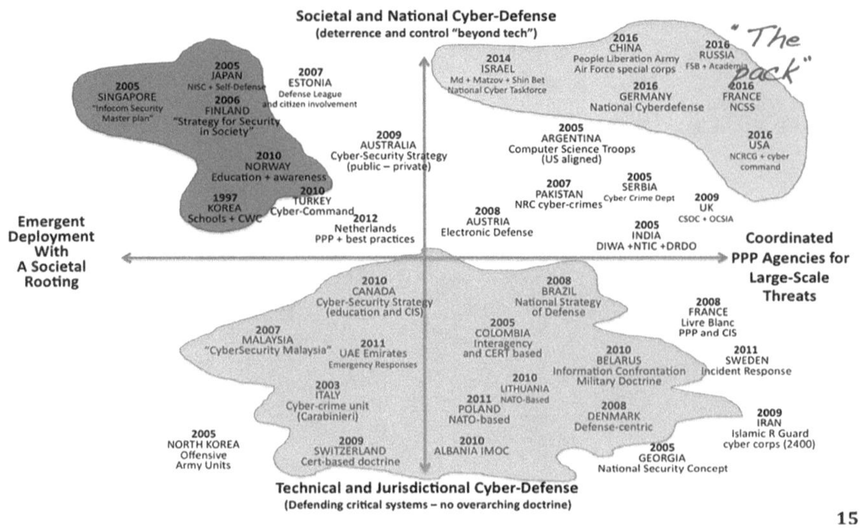

Fig. 4.4 Three groups of national cyberstrategies

national strategies' assumptions. This may be driven by the transposition of the principles of military capabilities escalation (weapons race, concentration, decisive capacities) to the tackling of cyber-criminality. Cybernetic offensive capabilities do not respond to traditional escalation and reinforcement models. They derive their malevolent capabilities from their transformational nature, their distributed deployment, and their superior and autonomous learning.

4.2 Preventing Cyber-Attacks: Evolution and Technological Shifts

In order to conclude our study of *Cybersecurity in France,* we will, in this last section of the book, discuss in detail what could be the technological evolutions of the threat landscape in the years 2017–2030; and what it would mean for the design of the French national cyber security strategy.

This section will follow four steps:

- Describing how adversaries will evolve based on assumptions of the evolution of technology and society in the future;
- Try to understand how this evolution will transform into threats that are likely to emerge in the future;
- Describe what environment it will likely create;
- Try to draw some inferences concerning the required learning (and hence technology roadmap) we need to adopt to anticipate the above.

Our historical analysis of the evolution of cyber-threats (Chap. 2 of this book) suggested that *hacking* simultaneously gained in legitimacy, compliance and consistency over the years; while more and more escaping attribution. Hacking tools in 2017, such as the APT28 and APT29 software suites, are provided with a maintenance guarantee, an educational platform, a 24/7 customer support, and benefit from an open-source research which is much faster than any governmental secret lab. Adversaries will hence become in the future even more *unknown*, while being legitimate, compliant, congruous and consistent. Such adversaries will generate a specific new generation of threats, that we label "APNNC" for asymptomatic, patternless, no peak, no outlier and contrived. The rapid rise of artificial intelligence modeling tools, with the cheaper and more distributed computing power, will allow hacking groups' labs to embark and embed a more adaptive AI that will be able to hide its nominal patterns, generate new behavioral patterns that will be directly injected in the AI behavioral detection engines (causal attacks) so that every peak, every outlier, would be suppressed at the source. We call it a "contrived artificial intelligence" (Fig. 4.5).

This section is detailing the forthcoming fall of a dominant logic, *the fortress*, and attempts to explain from a technical point of view how this "signature paradigm" will collapse, and how a "behavioral intelligence" paradigm will substitute it in the forthcoming year.

4.2.1 A Critical Evolution of Threats: The Fall of the Signature Paradigm

A national strategy for cybersecurity must not only be compliant with the global state-of-the-art of computer security R&D, it ultimately needs to anticipate scientific research and technological advancements that may either *impede* or *transform* its organization. In this chapter, we will focus our attention on *targeted threats* in general, and *advanced persistent threats* in particular. While we are not putting aside the legitimate State and corporate efforts to contrive the growth of computer malware,

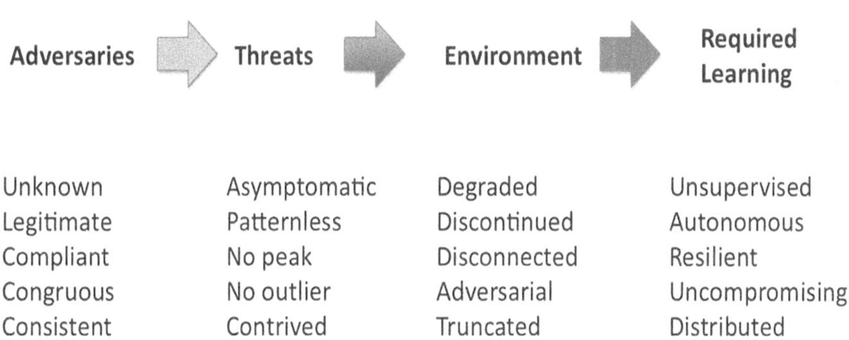

Fig. 4.5 The future of cyber warfare

we defend the perspective that targeted attacks gather most of the critical risks, on critical infrastructures, industries, the defense of civil liberties and sovereignty.

A malware is software that is intended to damage or disable a computer or a network system. This broad category includes viruses, Trojan horses, rootkits, but is mainly characterized by the absence of targeted knowledge (knowledge about a specific target), and the absence of persistence. Malwares are chunks of malicious code that originated in the early 1970s, with the exploratory and pioneering experiments of early-age hackers. Malwares can be automated, and even deploy a certain amount of automation and low-level procedural learning capabilities. For example, a code injection through a PDF file can also contain a code that erases its traces, by regenerating a clean PDF after the code injection.

Two approaches have been mainly used in the field of intrusion detection: misuse detection and anomaly detection. Misuse detection relies on the comparison of observed behaviors to pattern signatures of known attacks or intrusions. The systems based on this approach use a signature database. This kind of systems is the more commonly used, a good example being the snort tools. While it allows detecting accurately known attacks, the signatures are often generalized in order to detect the many variations of a given known attack. This leads to the increase of false positives (i.e. false alarms), as benign events can match a too generic attack signature. Systems based on the misuse approach are moreover unable to detect new and/or unknown intrusions that are not already present in the signature database. To detect new attacks, it is mandatory to keep the signature database up to date, which is a tremendous task.

Anomaly detection relies on the comparison of observed behaviors with a previously established "normal" behavior. Systems using this approach raise an alert when an observed behavior is sufficiently different from the normal behavior. It allows detecting new or unknown attacks, if these attacks imply an abnormal use of the system, which is generally the case. Most of the time, anomaly detection requires to explicitly building the model of normal behavior, either statically or dynamically (e.g., during a learning phase). This raises a problem: the model may be incomplete or incorrect, leading to false negatives (missing of attacks) or to false positives (false alarms).

Numerous approaches have been proposed to build the model of normal behavior: statistics, neural networks, naive Bayesian networks, Markov models, ad hoc models (e.g. sequences of system calls), etc. In current industry applications, external and ad hoc human interventions encounter scale, scope and skill obstacles. Signature-based intrusion detection systems (IDS) and malware protection software are dependent on accumulating very large database of known threats (signatures, behavior rules). Escalation of data collection damages productivity and escalates storage and maintenance costs for updating, through collection or algorithms, the most exhaustive description of malicious codes (cf. Table 4.1).

Targeted attacks are the entire contrary: they may, or they may not contain a malicious code. They may exploit "zero day" vulnerabilities, not as an end, but as a means to successfully conduct their objectives. They do not contain a single set of codes, but rather sophisticated and elaborated software that might encompass hundred thousand lines of codes.

Table 4.1 Signature versus behavioral paradigm

Strategic goals	Signature paradigm (hash)	Behavioral paradigm
Threats detection and analysis	• Malicious code identification is sufficient (CERT) • Vulnerable to zero-days • Undirected phishing attacks are the dominant logic	• Requires the identification of the Command and Control inside or outside of the network layer • Separating noise from traffic is challenging—statistical analysis
Attack attribution and situational awareness	• Detection of a malicious code does not precisely inform attribution	• Deep log analysis and log correlations (ex post)

Most importantly, a *human adversary* has designed them, which puts them closer to a weapon system than a computer virus. As such, targeted attacks are more likely to target a specific organization (e.g. a firm for industrial espionage and intellectual property theft, a State), gain a lasting foothold in the targeted environment, compromise a system for outreaching supra-ordinal goals (defense, destabilization, heist), and eventually, compromise sovereignty of a State.

With the rise of machine-to-machine communications and computer operations, the quest for secure machines and networks has become a core purpose in order to achieve the resilience of human societies, comprising their critical infrastructures, transport infrastructures and networks, financial investment markets, life support systems, aeronautical and defense systems and the secure pursuit of human activities. As the dependence on computers, machine-to-machine electronic and software components rises, so does the number of malicious and malevolent technical systems and individuals who try to intrude networks and systems in order to gain unauthorized access, conduct destructive operations, illegal intelligence gathering, or gain or elevate illicit privileges. Detecting, preventing and stopping such behaviors are respectively known as *computer security* and *network defense.*[2]

The arts of computer security and network defense rapidly evolved through the development of methods and systems to address the misuse and to deter intrusions in network systems.[3] Intrusion detection systems (IDS) provide computer and network defense mechanisms that identify the signatures of aberrant and unauthorized behavior within incoming traffic of data. Such systems are based on the detection of anomalies in comparison to *known* signatures or *known* normal behaviors and patterns.[4] Anomalies are deviations or departures from a normal or common order, form, pattern or rule. Anomaly detection consists of identifying significant statistical deviations of a data set from its supposed nominal distribution.[5]

---

[2]Bierly et al. (2008), Bourrier (1996), Fry et al. (2010), Kushner (2013), Roschlin and Meyer (1994).

[3]Parxson (1999), Sterbenz et al. (2010).

[4]Langner (2011), Li and Lai (2011).

[5]Al-Jarrah and Arafat (2014), Cheung et al. (2003), Cuppens and Miège (2002).

Table 4.2 Signature and behavioral paradigms in defensive goals

Defensive goals	Signature paradigm	Behavioral paradigm
Combating insider threats	• Detection of Man-in-the-Middle attacks—imposition of public key infrastructures—DNSSEC • Deterring browser hijackers	• APT is a prior mode of infiltration for organized crime. • Most favored mode of operations of States for infiltration (e.g. US TAO—Quantum attacks)
Protecting sovereignty	• Low probability of sovereignty risks	• High probability of governmental campaigns targeting sovereign assets
Resilient infrastructures and systems	• 2014 Black Energy malware targeting US infrastructures • DDoS attacks	• Advanced persistent malwares targeting intelligent and smart grids

Hence, the capacity of detecting anomalies depends on the prior knowledge and prior categorization of known threats, and their known signatures. Nominal distribution, however, is unknown in most typical applications or requires a nominal training data set in order to reliably estimate a normal or common order of test data.[6] This state of the art implies a constant quest for advancing the discovery and knowledge of known attacks and malicious behaviors, hence creating a competition for the development of detection methods of advanced attack and intrusion mechanisms that can escape the prior knowledge acquired by defense systems and methods[7] (Table 4.2).

Accordingly, offending and malicious systems have evolved in order to avoid pattern and signature recognition, and are known as "patternless intrusions", with their correspondent counter-systems known as "patternless intrusion detection systems". Such methods and systems attempt to address the rise of advanced and complex attacks, which rely on the combination of techniques allowing attackers to evade detection in order to gain and maintain a persistent access to the compromised network or system to finally conduct a series of operations that can include the retrieval of sensitive information stored electronically.[8]

This category of threats is known as "Advanced Persistent Threats" (APTs). Motives for APTs vary, and have included since their discovery: access to governmental files, technological and industrial espionage, illicit database retrieval on sensitive, strategic laboratories and monetary funds, tampering with strategic research programs, information on operational oil and gas field production, sabotaging competitive developments and political or commercial motives.[9]

National policies and national defense systems are heavily grounded in a shared understanding of what risks entail, and how they are composed. In France, as in

[6]Majorczyk et al. (2007), Manqui et al. (2010).

[7]Nelson (2010), Kloft and Laskov (2011), Olsavsky (2005).

[8]Liu et al. (2012), Sood et al. (2012), Virvilis et al. (2013).

[9]Kushner (2013), Lagner (2011).

Table 4.3 Static versus dynamic defense

	Static defense (Trust zones and privileges)	Dynamic defense (Deliberate ignorance of trust zones)
Signature paradigm	Defensive perspective Human bias in trust attribution "Fortress" philosophy Dependent on constant updating of external knowledge	Counter-defensive perspective Based on dynamic traffic inspection Favors software designed networks (SDN) Dependent on external sourcing for malicious code identification
Behavioral paradigm	Normative behavioral control replaces identification of malicious codes Baseline of "healthy" behaviors is difficult to establish Knowledge-based approach, relying on human teaching	Continuous and decentralized behavioral prediction ignores signatures and privilege levels Behavioral anomalies are detected as they occur, based on the continuous assessment of behavioral compliance Behavioral modeling approach based on ex ante professional expertise
Predictive AI paradigm	Predictive artificial Intelligence learns and predicts the overall transformation of the protected system	Predictive artificial intelligence learns the behavior of each machine component, through unsupervised and continuous learning

most G8 countries, the dominant logic is what we call the "signature paradigm". The signature paradigm is the design of network defense systems based on the identification and recognition of malicious code's signatures, obtained through traffic analysis and packet inspection. Such a paradigm implies a conception of defense inspired by its physicality: the network is seen as a fortress, with doors, gates, and firewalls, and accordingly, with a static perspective on authority and trust. Actors with privileges "within the walls" are granted more access and more rights than actors with lesser levels of trust and privileges (Table 4.3).

The above table describes the three competing paradigms for cybersecurity: the "signature paradigm", "the behavioral paradigm", and the "predictive AI paradigm". Most national strategies are grounded into a static defense perspective, based on signatures (top left corner). In the pursuit of this chapter, we will describe the technological innovations that are shaping the global R&D in defensive computer security (Behavioral and Predictive AI) paradigms, as to determine its consequences for policy making and national cyber-defense policies.

4.2.2 The Behavioral Paradigm: Patternless and Intelligent Behaviors

In the mid-2000s, research efforts took in consideration the forthcoming decay of a security paradigm based on signatures and traffic inspection. We identify this momentum as the rise of a "machine learning paradigm" in computer security. The main objective of this area of research is to allow the detection of a threat without the prior knowledge of a characterizing pattern, or without the detection of a malicious code (signature). Hence, "patternless Intrusion Detection Systems" (PIDS) rely on neither prior human behavior modeling nor signatures of malicious behaviors in order to detect an anomalous behavior.[10] Yet, they still rely on the detection of deviations or departures from a normal or common order, form, pattern or rule by interpreting a network behavior with a statistical analysis of observable network traffic.[11] PIDS consist of graphical use interfaces (GUIs) that allow visualizing a network's overall behavior, and thus, detecting abnormal or anomalous behavior within the network or system. This method depends on human expertise or network administrators with knowledge of the state of the art in order to decide if the observed traffic should be identified as anomalous.

The discovery of an anomaly in machine behavior involves being able to determine if the observed behavior is new to this machine and its operational environment. This task is known as novelty detection.[12] Novelty detection is the identification of a new or unknown data, signal, pattern, signature or behavior that machine learning has not previously learned or acquired either through training or through a discovery mechanism. Thus, novelty detection involves recognizing a signal that differs from previous signals, triggering an unexpected perception.[13] Typical approaches involve creating a novelty filter by learning a data set that describes normal data, signals, behaviors or signatures.[14] Human beings, i.e. users, network administrators, or experts in the concerned field for novelty detection, typically train these data sets. Once acquired, this training is applied to new signals in order to determine if the incoming data or signal presents unknown characteristics to the novelty filter data set.

The vulnerability of such approaches is known as the problem of "unknown unknowns": the novelty detection filter is limited to datasets that are known in advance. Patterns, signals or signatures that do not fall in known classes, categorizations or patterns, cannot be determined as "new" or "unknown" to the specific training of the novelty detection filter. Hence, a signal can be "unknown" to a specific training data set, but not new. Inversely, a signal can present characteristics known to the training data set, while offering a combination of data that is new. Novelty detection systems are known for presenting this vulnerability of depending on prior learning that can accurately describe their fault conditions.

Several approaches allow circumscribing "*unknown unknowns*" circularity. Statistical approaches to novelty detection are based on modeling the statistical properties of known normal behavior, signals or signatures, and confronting new data set with a preexisting model of the "known".

---

[10]Nelson (2010), Olsavsky (2005).

[11]Ou et al. (2009), Oslavsky (2005).

[12]Markou and Singh (2003).

[13]Marsland (2003).

[14]Roberts and Tarassenko (1994).

Such techniques involve computing the density function of a known data class, the statistical distance between known data models and new data, or differences in data characteristics, such as frequency compared to known frequencies, peak behavior compared to known peak behaviors and data neighboring compared to usual neighboring.

However, in a typical real world situation, data, signals or signatures are only not always known or captured in full, and therefore, their underlying distribution, peak behaviors, neighbors and parameters are unknown to the receiving machine, unless taught from external sources with a specific teaching mechanism. In case of lack of prior knowledge, normative approaches fail to recognize if a pattern could be deemed as unknown or known.[15]

Another *parametric* approach to novelty detection involves calculating the rejection rate of an incoming set of data, assuming that data distributions are Gaussian in nature. This approach is known as the "error-rejection trade off" between the data being recognized and the data being rejected.[16] However, such an approach is based on the codification or classification of human confidence in the rules that are used for classifying the data. Hence, this approach does not solve the "unknown unknowns" obstacle, and may, on the contrary, increase the rate of false negatives as it involves, in typical situations, dropping estimates based on a posteriori probabilities.

Another set of approaches to detect novelty use probabilistic and Bayesian techniques. They are known as Gaussian Mixture Modeling (GMM). The typical technique in these approaches consists of maximizing the log likelihood of the training data with optimization algorithms.[17] The method consists of building a heuristic model in order to *minimize* the number of thresholds in the novelty detection system.

Such techniques are appropriate when a *very large number* of events are accessible to train and refine the model. The approach consists of building a large statistical model of normality, and testing, then refining the heuristics of discovery against this model. This approach is well adapted to "*knowable unknowns*", i.e. to discover unexpected variations or evolutions of data in a data set with a prior knowledge of its usual patterns of behaviors, and has been successfully used in the domains of medicine diagnostic, jet engine fault detection or similar domains with important flows of statistical data over a known and comparable population of events.

The probabilistic discovery of novelty has been used in computer intrusions detection in an approach known as Hidden Markov Models (HMM). The approach consists of teaching a system with a finite number of states that are not observable by the system. The transition between one state to another is considered a stochastic process. The method calculates the probability of transition for each state, and compares it to the modeling of normal system behavior. For instance, system call sequences and shell command sequences can be modeled into a hidden normal

---

[15]Markou and Singh (2003), Ou et al. (2009), Oslavsky (2005).

[16]Chow (1970), Hansen et al. (1997).

[17]Roberts and Tarassenko (1994).

Table 4.4 Three generations of threats and deterrence strategies

	Known unknowns	Knowable unknowns	Unknowns unknowns
Learning	Incident learning and signature sharing (databases: Kapersky, FireEye, Symantec, etc.)	PIDS—patternless learning. Even if the attack is unknown, the deviations it creates can be observed	HMM or GMM—Heuristic models that limit the number of thresholds in novelty detection—Unsupervised learning
Detection	Recognition of signatures or hashes Statistical inference from known signatures (derivations)	Anomaly is detected by seeking outliers in the outputs of the learned or trained model (human supervision)	Anomaly of behaviors are tested against the autonomous internal learning of every behaviors (known or unknown)
Limitations	*What you don't know will hurt you* Numerous false positives	*Learning circularity*: low intensity attacks, or compliant attacks (insider threat) are undetected	Requires dynamic baselines and recurrent updating. Not tolerant to vertical architectures (learning must be preserved)
Deterrence	Attackers are identified by the Indicators of compromise and malicious codes they leave behind	Attackers can be detected even if they do not use malicious code (or known code) but prone to false negatives	Autonomous defense: every decentralized component has its own artificial intelligence to develop a local situational awareness

behavior and an expectation-maximization (EM) algorithm can be used to detect a novel behavior in the data set.[18]

Such an approach compares the probability distribution of a normal system over time with the frequency distribution of incoming behaviors. However, modeling data distributions in advance, and then estimating the probability of a deviation from the known probabilities of distribution of these behaviors drives typical methods (see Table 4.4). Such methods do not achieve an autonomous learning of novelty detection, as novelty criteria have to be discovered before applying the novelty detection model.[19]

Such methods are efficient for the recognition of *known symptoms* within large data sets, for instance when an important class of symptom is under-represented in a data set. Hence, novelty detectors always rely on previously taught data, signals or behaviors that are inconsistent with the remainder of the known dataset, and thus, are incapable of detecting novelty without the existence of a prior model of "normal" data, signals or behaviors. Consistent with this perspective, most nations develop computer emergency response teams (CERTs), which conduct continuous threat analysis based on the collection of threat intelligence.

[18]Yeung and Ding (2002).

[19]Markou and Singh (2003).

National CERTs collect data from public, private and governmental databases used as repositories of known threats and their signatures. A signature can either be constituted of an algorithm (i.e. a description of a malevolent behavior, either rule-based or pattern-based) or a hash value of a known malevolent code. A hash value (or *hash*) is derived from a string of bytes, which uniquely identify a specific malware. Most scanners hence rely on the similarity or variations of existing malevolent codes. The performance of scanning signatures depends on the ex ante knowledge of kernel, CPU, bytecode or script instructions, known to be nefarious.

As hashes are commonly one-way reduction algorithms, they may perform a partial capture of an injected malevolent code, and can be prone to either false negatives or false positives. There is no guarantee that a certain byte sequence is unique, which leads most detection engines to rely on in-house algorithms that automatically generate large arrays of variations of known signatures. Consequently, more vendors are proliferating signatures at the rate of 600–900,000 samples per day, which increases the rate of false positives. On the attack side, experience attackers eventually generate malware code that has been morphed to escape known signature-based detection algorithms, which can make them undetectable until a specific algorithm from one of the vendors is able to identify the modification. Hence, most static detection is a continuous cloak and dagger game, where the shield never really catches up with the continuous metamorphosis of the daggers (Table 4.5).

Table 4.5 Computational limitations of PIDS and HM

	Characteristics	Implications for policy and national cyberdefense
PIDS	Detection of deviations from a "discovered" nominal order Statistical analysis of "observable" traffic Implies the use of human expertise to detect and point out abnormal patterns	Requires continuous and very large scale monitoring (interception, violation of privacy rights) Does not resolve the problem of "unknown unknowns" (zero day attacks) Weak on novelty detection; would require deep learning on a very large scale
Error-Rejection Trade off and GMM	Use of Gaussian distribution models applied to traffic analysis Vulnerable to the level of human confidence in pre-established rules May increase the rate of false negatives	Overly centralized approach involves building very large scale intrusion systems May defeat the initial purpose by revealing overall vulnerabilities of the defense system Requires a known and comparable population of events (logs)
HMM	Does not address the issue of unrepresentative data Requires the creation of a normative base line Fails to discover novel behaviors	At a national level, use of HMM would require intensive computation capabilities and very large initial base lines. The approach is not appropriate for the detection of dynamic and metamorphic threats

In particular, such methods have difficulties handling "unrepresentative data", i.e. data that fails to display characteristics that would allow attributing them a typical deviation from normal behavior. Generally, when confronted with such "unrepresentative data", novelty detection simply ignores them. This is a common problem in outlier detection. The current state of the art in anomaly detection recurrently stumbles on this obstacle, failing to produce a satisfying answer with methods based on nominal distributions and prior normative learning. The following table summarizes these technological evolutions, and discusses their implications for policy and the adaptation of national cybersecurity strategies.

4.2.3 Predictive Artificial Intelligence and Incongruity Detection

A critical issue for policy-makers and designers of national cyber-security defense systems lies in novelty detection and unrepresentative data. As we underlined earlier in this monograph, advanced persistent threats (APTs) do not rely on a typical codes, and may not use an archetypical set of malicious codes. From an historical perspective, on the contrary, most large scale APTs were relying of legitimate coding, substituting astute automated learning, and exploiting zero-day vulnerabilities.

Sigmund Freud conducted one of the first studies of a discovery mechanism dealing with "unrepresentative data" (1905). Freud suggested that humor is derived from the release of an unconscious—suppressed of forbade—content, by an utter incongruity that brings it to consciousness. In this perspective, the receiver is not aware of these unconscious processes, yet he or she builds a framework of interrelations that have their own intrinsic harmony.[20] "Incongruous" information, in this definition, is a combination of data that is not in agreement or dramatically lacks harmony with the internal and unaware logic of the receiver. In Freud's perspective, the "unaware state" of this internal logic is not automatic, but maintained by suppression or self-deceit mechanisms, which are part of inhibition. Hence, to self-reveal this unconscious relation presents a psychological expenditure for the bearer. For Freud, the pleasure in jokes "arises from an economy in expenditure upon inhibition" (1905).

Thus, following Freud's definition, an *incongruity* can arise without the presence of a prior and explicitly agreed normal order of information between an emitting and a receiving party. Incongruity is produced by the incompatibility between an *internal logic* and *external stimuli* that are inconsistent with this internal logic.

This method of measuring discordance is advantageous over "anomaly detection" methods, which require the measurement of deviation from a known or normal order, pattern or organization of behavior and data. Incongruous data, stimulus, events or behaviors are data, stimuli, events or behaviors that are not in

[20] Freud (1905): pp. 147–149.

accord with the specific expectation derived from the internally "learned" logic of the receiver.

Rauterberg (1995) defines incongruity as "the difference between internal complexity of a learning system and external complexity of the context". However, such a definition does not encompass the possibility of "self-incongruity", that is to say the state of incongruity of a system, a reasoning model, and a "worldview" without the need to confront it with other systems, models or worldviews. Freud's perspective separating the implicit (unconscious) habitual mental picture compared to the explicit (revealed or self-revealed) presents the advantage of integrating an autonomous perspective in incongruity detection.

Freud's perspective offers the advantage of exploring the discovery of an internal incongruity by the system producing or carrying this incongruity itself. Shultz (1972) proposed a definition of incongruity that is more compatible with Freud's original perspective, by defining it as "the simultaneous presence of two or more habitually incompatible elements, where an element can be either an object or an event".

Hence, an incongruity can be derived or discovered by the introduction of a new element (novelty), or simply, by the discovery of an unsuspected relation between elements that were already known (self-revelation). Dissonance can be the result of a confrontation between an internal expectation and information coming from the external environment, as much as a discordance between internal relations between events that suddenly come to the awareness of perceiver or perceiving system.

The theory of incongruity has known few developments outside the field of study of humor. The mechanism of incongruity discovery has itself drawn little attention in the art. Miller et al. (1960: p. 26) proposed a perspective on the role of incongruity in cybernetics (in: *Plan and Structure of Behavior*). They inferred that the response of effectors to an event depends on testing, then re-testing operational procedures while watching how these iterations "modify the outcome of the test" (p. 25): "The action is initiated by an "incongruity" between the state of the organism and the state that is being tested for, and the action persists until the incongruity (i.e., the proximal stimulus) is removed" (op. cit., p. 26). They called this initial model the "cybernetic hypothesis".

Morreall (1987) further proposed that incongruity resolution is not systematically followed by a negative reaction or a surprise, but can also be followed by reality assimilation. Morreall underlines that the discovery of an incongruity can serve the purpose of explaining and learning a new relation between two concepts or events, while assuming and accepting that they are incongruent.

This suggestion is important as it provides a cue for modeling the steps followed by the discoverer of an incongruous behavior, event or stimulus. In a similar approach than Miller et al. (1960), Morreall suggests that a an incongruity perceived for the first time will trigger an attempt to explain its possibility, trying to find rationales to make it more congruous to what the perceiver previously learned. Instead of reacting negatively or by rejection, perceivers try to "solve the problem", utilizing what they learned in the past about the relations between the incongruous display of events to try to make sense of them. Hence, Morreall proposed that incongruity is a trigger for sensemaking and curiosity.

4.2.4 The Elaboration of the First Incongruity Threat Intelligence Model

Jones (1975) introduced an application of the incongruity theory to the field of intelligence and threats deterrence. Jones suggested that the mechanisms of incongruity detection and production have been intensively used in warfare in order to deceive opponents, or to detect potential deceptions from malevolent opponents.

By analyzing war events, Jones concluded that the mechanism of incongruity is of relative nature. Following Freud, Jones suggested that incongruity occurred when there was a *mismatch* or *discordance* between an expected organization or order of signals, and the internal logic of the receiver, but this "internal consistency or logic" of the receiver could not be measured, guessed or approximated from a known and objective outside order.

Consistency and consonance, in Jones' perspective, are constructs that individuals and organizations build over time through their personal and specific experiences. Therefore, Jones inferred, the objective of the intelligence work is to discover the specific and idiosyncratic "logic" of the receiver, in order to anticipate what the target receiver might conceive as congruous or incongruous with his or her own logic of perception. Such an approach had not been experimented with machine learning in general, and not explored in the context of two machines interacting with each other.

Jones advanced the art a step forward by suggesting a transitive processing rule in the handling of congruities and incongruities. When an incongruity is expected, and an incongruity is delivered, the interaction between two entities will be deemed "congruous", as expectation is matched with the received data, signal or behavior. Therefore, a congruity can be "unexpected" (Jones 1975: p. 12) if the receiving organization, individual or unit is expecting a high level of incongruity from its interacting party. As Jones noted: "Yet a further variant is where the incongruity is actually created by the occurrence of a *congruity* where an incongruity would have been normally expected" (ibid*)*. If an operational environment is expected to be turbulent and then displays a sudden quietness, or the emission of unexpectedly compliant signals from the source, a human observer will interpret it as a strong anomaly. This behavioral pattern is typical of insider's threat behavior. For instance, a bank clerk that is suddenly becoming overly quiet, from the point of view of its network activity and logs, may signal an undetected deviation in his or her behavior. Bank cyber-heists are prone to this type of low signals, as insiders, highly knowledgeable of the bank practices, over-do the broadcast of compliant signals.

The 2016 Bangladesh bank heist is a fair example of this "incongruity expectation", and of the manipulation of fabricated incongruity to deceit a surveillance system. In February 2016, hackers, ordering the Federal Bank of New York to transfer, via a SWIFT order, to transfer $951 million to several accounts, issued five transactions.

Insiders sought the best calendar date, and the best hour, to send the SWIFT instructions, from Bangladesh to New York to further credit accounts in the

Philippines. Although the heist did not completely succeeded, hackers were able to grab $81 million that were credited by the Philippine banking system to an account with Rizal Bank, and "eventually withdrawn".[21] Hackers launched their heist when the bank was closed (February 5 and 8, 2016). They knew that the amount of compliance controls will be lower, and they knew where and how the approval circuit would occur. When a bank is closed, *incongruity* would be expected, as normal approval processes would not be in place. Hence, hackers deployed what Jones labeled a "contrived incongruity" strategy, i.e. crafting a level of incongruity that would be tolerated and *foreseen* as "normal" by the controlling authority.[22]

Albeit, the hackers did not expect that a physical flaw in the printer of the Bangladesh bank. As reported by Yap and Calonzo: "Zubair Bin Huda, a joint director of Bangladesh Bank, found the printer tray empty when he looked on the morning of February 5 for confirmations of SWIFT financial transactions that are normally printed automatically overnight" (ibid.). He tried to understand what happened by retrieving the operations manually in the SWIFT system. Bin Huda reported the incident to the Police. "We thought it was a common problem just like any other day," Huda said in the complaint[23] (ibid.). A typo in the beneficiary's name confirmed the suspicions of a fraudulent operation.

Jones inferred that incongruities are thus *neither objective, nor detected from are statistical deviations* or departures from a priory known normal or common order, form, pattern or rule. Each unit, human being, organization constructs its own set of expected rules and relations between events, and the latter can only be known through interacting with the potential entities that will receive a congruous or incongruous signal.

In the Bangladesh's central bank cyber-heist, the criminal gang opened five bank accounts before hand with Philippines' Rizal Commercial Banking Corp (RCBC), belonging to fictitious identities. "The funds were transferred to a foreign exchange broker for conversion into pesos, transferred back to RCBC and consolidated into the bank account of a Chinese-Filipino businessman".[24] The money laundering operation was also designed in the plan, allowing to then transfer the funds to three casinos in the Philippines, converting them into chips, and then reconverting them

---

[21]Yap and Calonzo (2016).

[22]"The hackers chose the weekend in four countries as the opportune moment to break into the BB system. The weekly two-day bank holiday starts in Bangladesh at Thursday midnight and a day later in the US, the Philippines and Sri Lanka. Knowing that there would be no mutual correspondence immediately, around the midnight on February 4, a Thursday, the hackers sent the fake payment orders.", *Asian News,* R.K. Byron and Md F. Rahman, "Hackers bugged Bangladesh Bank system in Jan", March 11, 2016.

[23]"Because it was a Friday—a weekend in Muslim-majority Bangladesh—Huda left the office around 11.15 am and asked colleagues to help fix the problem. It took them more than 24 h before they could manually print the receipts, which revealed dozens of questionable transactions that sent the bank racing to stop cash from leaving its account with the Federal Reserve Bank of New York to the Philippines, Sri Lanka and beyond", C. Yap and A. Calonzo, op. cit.

[24]Byron (2016).

in cash transfers to a Hong Kong bank.[25] In order to decoy the central bank's standard operational procedures, the hacker group intruded the bank's network as to observe how bank employees crafted their messages, how they replied to protocol's requests. Hence, both the initial intrusion and the on-going social engineering that preceded the hack were undetected by anomaly detectors. The hackers involved in the heist insured that their behavior would be *compliant* with operational procedures, and *congruent* to both expectations of surprise (i.e. special protocols on national holidays), and "congruous within the incongruous"!

Whether a receiver will consider an event or signal, as "incongruous" will therefore depend on of the "mental picture" he or she holds about the emitter of such a signal or event. However, this "picture", "belief" or "representation" is constructed through interacting with the emitter, and there dynamically evolves over time.

People measure incongruity relatively to what they have learned about their interlocutors' behaviors, and judge new behaviors relatively to the past knowledge they accumulated through interactions. Evaluating incongruity hence depends both on the knowledge of the interlocutor, self-knowledge (knowledge of own behavior), and evaluating if a new interaction is harmonious or disharmonious, consistent or inconsistent, in consonance or in dissonance, with previous interactions.

Jones (1975) further introduced the notions of "preparation and induction" in producing unnoticed incongruities before they become apparent. For Jones, incongruities are detected according to their relative dissonance with the "congruity versus incongruity" expectations of the victim. There is therefore a method to diminish the *relative* incongruity's weight of an event by adjusting its perceived incongruous value over time.

In other words, if an incongruity is introduced *slowly* over time by small steps presenting a low relative incongruity value, there is a probability that this incongruity will not be considered intolerable at each step, while growing unnoticed in the perception framework of the victim. I hacker's terms, this would mean defeating the work factor analysis of the adversary, by injecting false flags (or tempered probe data) to deceive the WFA engine of the targeted network defense.[26] The following table summarizes the role played by congruity and incongruity in the Bangladesh's central bank cyber-heist (Table 4.6).

As we will see in the next section, the concept of *incongruity detection* is central to the future of threat intelligence. Normative and nominal learning fail because most adversaries perfectly master the art of "feeding" a normative detection probe. Moreover, anomaly detection is highly societal: even a mathematician who is designing a rule-based anomaly detection engine does it with societal assumptions of what is "normal" or "not normal". Human beings, in the future, will not be

[25]According to Byron, op. cit., "*The funds were converted into pesos in various tranches to the bank accounts of Chinese national Weikang Xu, Eastern Hawaii Leisure Co and Bloomberry Hotels Inc (Solaire Resorts)*".

[26]Such a preparation would consist of designing and crafting signals or behaviors so that they contrive a higher relative congruity value that intrinsic incongruous value to the receiver.

Table 4.6 Jones incongruity framework applied to cyber-security

Jones incongruity theory	Definition	Examples in the Bangladesh case study
Manufactured congruity	Signals are sent to the target match its expectations of the emitter's behavior	Hackers learned the verbose, the language used by employees when reacting to unexpected protocol requests
Contrived incongruity	The adequate level of "expected incongruity" is broadcasted to the target	Hackers waited for a national holiday to benefit from a more tolerable environment to the incongruity of their demands
Dissonance reduction (preparation)	Acclimatization of victims' expectations by introducing small incongruities over time (increase tolerance)	The money laundering network is settled before the heist and embedded in several transactions
"Incongruity simple"	A mismatch between an expected behavior and its materialization, both foreign to existing explicative models, and in value	The empty printer tray that led the transactions to go through without being printed (and hence controlled). This incongruity foiled the further heist of $870 millions

capable of competing with machine intelligence. To pursue the design of anomaly detection solely based on human expertise is therefore purely suicidal.

Moreover, societies will develop a high tolerance for "unknown" counter-parts in everyday transactions. The development of digital currencies will transform electronic commerce, and globally raise the tolerance for "unknown" interlocutors and transactions. This societal trend will transform in a much higher societal tolerance for *anything ephemeral*, but not "ephemeral" as understood by the sociologists of the 1990s; *truly ephemeral* in that sense that many human transactions will be conducted with ephemeral identities, situational currencies (currencies that are valid for only a set of purposes for a limited time, which will be developed around 2025 to fight against a rampant global organized crime).

A society that would have been overexposed, and over-traumatized by many political turnarounds in Europe and in the United States, will value privacy and discretion in the future. Social exposure trends (Facebook, Twitter) will reverse, and will create a demand for *societal discretion*. Ephemeral and disposable identities will be the solution.

The only detection capability that would be left will be *behavioral intelligence*, and at its core, the capability to model in real time, from raw data captured by intelligent sensors, any human and machine behavior. The following section explores the creation of such intelligent sensors.

4.3 Exploring Counter-Measures to Defeat AI Campaigns

The main technical challenge of artificial intelligence attack campaigns resides in detecting the presence and a malicious, hazardous or malevolent activity, even after their first intrusion was successful and undetected. However, knowledge-based and behavior-based intrusion detection systems are *not* designed to support ongoing operations after a system has been compromised.[27] The objective of such methods is to grant a machine or a user with a permission, which covers a range of legitimate and authorized behaviors.

As such methods rely on prior knowledge, deviations or departures from normal behaviors, once the permission is obtained, the intruding software or attacker can legitimately engage in unsuspected activities, such as granting itself other permissions, given they are in the range of approved behaviors by the signature-based or behavior-based detection system. Such vulnerability is known for creating overall resilience threat[28] as they create environments with persistent degraded security that can be exploited by the attackers. Furthermore, as "dormant" or undetected Advanced Persistent Threat propagated within a target network or system, the overall vulnerability of the network or system increases in unknown proportions.

Advanced Persistent Threats follow typical steps for intrusion and operation.[29] These typical steps resemble what Jones described (1978) when he observed field agents gathering intelligence and intruding targets' organizations during war events. They unfold as follows: In a first step, the attacker conducts a reconnaissance exploration. This exploration aims at identifying the defense and network configurations of the targeted network or system.

This first step, in Jones' perspective, would correspond to the period during which the emitter of a decoy or deception builds a fact sheet of the target's expectations of congruous and incongruous behaviors. In particular, in computer attacks, perpetrators would try to identify the shape of the targeted network or system, its port of entries, its protocols, its certification and signature processes, its known and reputable users, its revision and back-up routines, in order to determine the method of entry that would be the most probable to avoid detection.

In a second step, the attacker intrudes the targeted system through a communication device or a communication agent delivery, hoping to be unnoticed. When intrusion is successful, the targeted system is "compromised".

In a third step, the software agent of the attacker, or the attacker himself, now resident in the targeted host system, collects data and information about the expectations of the system regarding legitimate, authentic and authorized operations (making itself *congruent* to system expectations). This data, contrary to traditional attacks, is not communicated outside of the host target system, in order to prevent detection and to maintain the intruder unnoticed by behavior-based detection

[27]Garfinkel and Dinolt (2011).

[28]Sterbenz et al. (2010), Fry et al. (2010).

[29]Li and Lai (2011), Sood and Enbody (2012).

systems. This third step is used as to locally, from within the targeted host system, create false evidence of genuine signatures, certificates that might be used by knowledge-based detection systems.

In a fourth step, the propagation and activation of the intruded software is triggered autonomously, through different techniques that can include a previously set timer, an event-based triggering routine, or a simple random algorithm (reducing the detection of an internal incongruous behavior). The intruded software agent can then trigger a synchronization and outbound communication routine, as to inform the attack perpetrator of the success of the operation, collect and gather sensitive information, collect and reveal to the attacker critical vulnerabilities of target, etc.

The objective of Advanced Persistent Threats (APTs) attacks is to compromise a network or local system without being detected, in order to achieve partial or total ownership of its command and control. Once this partial ownership is achieved, an APT can autonomously take control of targeted network resources, upload codes and programs, implement false evidence, access sensitive data, implement dormant software for delayed or autonomously triggered malicious attacks, and, finally escape the host system without having been detected.

To avoid detection, Advanced Persistent Threats use a combination of several techniques in order to change their behavior at each step of programmed behavior. This behavior of Advanced Persistent Threats is known as “morphing” or “situational adaptation”, which consists of changing the behavior of an attack while this attack is deploying. The first step, which consists of the attacker learning about the network or system defense, is critical for the success of APT attacks, as reconnaissance operation allows preparing to later morph itself “on the fly” in order to bypass both normative behavior-based and knowledge-based (signatures) detection systems. APTs that proceed to retrieve sensitive data and send them back to the attacker need, furthermore, to be able to exit the targeted network or system undetected.

4.3.1 APT Technological Locks and Defensive Strategy Implications

Several techniques are explored in the art to prevent such morphing.[30] A method could consist of modifying the predicaments and configurations of the targeted networks, hosts and applications continuously, following a pattern of modification that is unpredictable and undetectable by the APT attacker. Such a dynamic modification would be intended to confuse attackers, and to dynamically change the configuration of the compromised network so that automatic triggers of APTs would fail to operate properly would be eventually delayed or detected.

The rationale between these methods lies in the delay between the reconnaissance step, and the actual attack step, that the attackers would require to prepare and

[30]Ou et al. (2009).

Table 4.7 Comparing jones model with hacker's practice

	Reconnaissance	Intrusion	Compromise
Jones contrived incongruity elaboration (1975)	Attackers learn the target's psychology and modus operandi	Attackers defeat the target's sensor through decoy	Attacker tries to be "congruous" with target's expectations
Hacker's modus operandi	Looking for open ports, preparatory social engineering	Credentials theft, target impersonation, spear phishing	Counter-WFA: attackers try to defeat probe by feeding them with compliant behaviors

induce the targeted network or system. However, this method would not allow detecting a dynamically contrived incongruous behavior.

The method would dynamically change the targeted environment intruded by the attacker, hoping that such a disturbance would impede the attack's success, without knowing the shape of this attack, and without being able to locate where the attack is actually taking place. Moreover, such a method would be impractical and would not trigger successful outcomes when a network or system has already been compromised, as the APT intruder would already benefit from approved signatures, authorizations and security level permits, that it would eventually uses to dynamically adapt to the morphing of the network or system (see Table 4.7).

Even in the case of dynamic address or port hopping, that is to say dynamically changing the addresses used by a protocol or a program, an APT intruder that has already compromised the targeted network would be able to learn from inside the dynamic hopping, and would, therefore, further increasing its penetration in the network. Furthermore, when an APT attack is in its final phase of exiting the system with retrieved confidential and sensitive data, it is likely going to use legitimate port of communications, and/or legitimate protocols to achieve its external communication. Yet, legitimate users of the targeted network need to be able to use these outbound communication ports for their daily use. Therefore, the constant and dynamic morphing of the targeted network will make sure that these legitimate outbound communication channels are always available, and hence could be use by an exiting APT (Table 4.8).

Hence, detecting and preventing Advanced Persistent Threats involves detecting an *incongruous behavior* of a machine or network component inbound (as the attacker's software intrudes the system), and outbound (when the attacker's software leaves the system). Therefore, adversarial reconnaissance can be operated in the preparation phase (first step of APT), as well as during the other phases (two to five) of an APT, and during its exiting behavior.

Table 4.8 Defeating artificial intelligence

	Reconnaissance	Intrusion	Compromise
Intelligent (AI) attacks	Bots and dynamic probing of targeted network as to identify easiest point of entry	AI engine observe and learns interactions before impersonating a false user	Trigger-based sleeping protocols: triggered only when conditions are met
Traditional techniques to defeat intelligent attacks	Morphing the network: remapping and reallocating resources continuously	Dynamic privileges with continuous renewal of credentials	Code reverse engineering, obfuscation and "live testing" of functions (KPI)
Limitation	Address hoping and counter-morphing can be learned by an AI engine	Human error: defense systems are vulnerable to the "master key" syndrome	An obfuscated triggered-based intelligent malware is nearly unbeatable (until it activates itself)

4.3.2 *Helping Machines to Detect Their Own Incongruous Behaviors*

Measuring the "self-congruity" or "self-incongruity" of a network or system behavior would advantageously allow detecting and measuring an incongruous behavior, whether or not the network or system environment is morphing. The use of relative behavioral modeling, that is to say modeling on the fly the behavior of software, components, data and events relatively to previous behaviors and previous interactions, allows to focus on the detection of interrelated behavioral changes of machines and components through the calculation of relative values.

The use of relative frequencies of modification, instead of comparison with normative and fixed values, allows following the transformation of a targeted behavior, before, during and after an interaction. This method allows learning adaptively and integrating the overall dynamic change of a target environment.[31]

A successful detection of an Advanced Persistent Threat behavior thus requires being able to detect and measure the incongruity of an *external event* (a machine-to-machine communication, a network event, for example), and simultaneously and relatively, estimating the "self-congruity" or "self-incongruity" of the targeted system of machine itself.

Successful detection requires both the ability to develop a situational awareness of incoming events, and a self-awareness of changes taking place in the local behavior of the host or potentially threatened machine or node. The combination of these two learning principles would ensure to predict outcomes before they occur, by anticipating the expected behavior towards a previously learned incongruous

[31]Following Jones (1975) elaboration of the relativity of congruity and incongruity.

behavior, either from a machine-to-machine interaction, or at locally and endogenously to a specific node.

If Advanced Persistent Threats follow established steps of reconnaissance, infiltration, legitimating, executing and exiting, they can encompass, as a class of behavior; and many different stratagems exist, with the use of a large variety of techniques at each step.[32] Juels and Yen underline that the versatility and the important range of behaviors and tactics involved in APTs would be more appropriately described as "campaigns" than as "programs". This versatility makes APT's class of attack behaviors difficult to identify or declare as such, as some of these tactics may not involve any illegitimate techniques.

For example, an APT conducted by a legitimate insider may use several authorized behaviors, bearing signatures, and granted access, given that the perpetrator is, from the start, an identified and accredited user of the system. This property of APTs constitutes a challenge as their behaviors cannot be related to a specific prior knowledge, a specific component usage, a specific address or port hopping, a specific signature, etc. The challenge proposed is therefore similar the challenges that Jones' field agents had to face[33]: to use a combination of hunches, guessing, intuition, code-level tools, exploratory testing, signals detection instruments, to build judgments about a potential intrusion and a potential stratagem of attackers, leading, eventually, to the discovery of an Advanced Persistent Threat. Scenario recognition is hence a difficult challenge to solve.[34]

4.3.3 The Rise of Artificial Intelligence and Incongruity Detection

The number of "APT-related" incidents in the years 2011–2017 increased to such a level that many of these attack campaigns could no longer be labeled as APT. The most advanced of these campaigns, such as Careto,[35] Duqu[36] in 2011, Flame in 2012, Regin[37] in 2014, Equation[38] in 2015 and Project Sauron (Strider)[39] in 2016, securely escape most of the state-of-the-art detection techniques. These new generations of attacks are characterized by an intensive use of zero day exploits, extremely innovative persistence techniques, and benefit from truly advanced programming framework.

[32]Juels and Yen (2012).

[33]Jones (1978).

[34]Cheung et al. (2003).

[35]https://securelist.com/blog/research/58254/the-caretomask-apt-frequently-asked-questions/.

[36]https://securelist.com/blog/incidents/32463/duqu-faq-33/.

[37]https://securelist.com/blog/research/67741/regin-nation-state-ownage-of-gsm-networks/.

[38]https://securelist.com/blog/research/68750/equation-the-death-star-of-malware-galaxy/.

[39]https://securelist.com/analysis/publications/75533/faq-the-projectsauron-apt/.

As noted by the Kapersky's advanced research group on APT (GReAT), Project Sauron use the latest encryption algorithms, "steals encryption keys, configuration files, and IP addresses of the key infrastructure servers related to the encryption software",[40] uses "legitimate software distribution channels for lateral movement within infected networks" and controls its own dissemination to specific geographical locations.[41]

The striking characteristic of this new generation of attack vectors is that they have been designed to defeat *automation*, while using autonomous machine learning to dynamically adapt to their targets. As noted by Kapersky Labs, "Almost all of ProjectSauron's core implants are unique, have different file names and sizes, and are individually built for each target" (*ibid.).* Code is regenerated for each attack campaign in order to avoid signature detection. Low-bandwidth mode is triggered as to minimize the incongruity of the broadcasting activity. The platform has its own high-level language, allowing scripting its own protocols, and its own DNS tunnels. As put by Kapersky in its 2017 annual report: "Clues are dead".[42] As noted by the authors: "Indicators of Compromise (IoCs) have long been an excellent way of sharing traits of known malware, allowing defenders to recognize an active infection. The discovery by GReAT of the ProjectSauron APT changed this. Analysis of the threat actor group revealed a bespoke malware platform where every feature was altered for each victim, rendering IoCs unreliable for detecting any other victim, unless accompanied by another measure."[43]

The automation and the autonomy of a threat intelligence that would support the detection of intrusions is hence a recurrent challenge for the art. Automation does not necessarily involve *autonomous* learning and autonomy does not necessarily involve *automated* learning. Behavior-based intrusion detection systems can automate their analysis of a behavior, and search for differences with "healthy behaviors". But the knowledge of "healthy behaviors" typically requires than it was taught to the behavior-based detection algorithm before hand.

When no prior teaching is required, such Behavior-based detection systems still typically relies on the comparison of data with nominal distributions, Gaussian distributions, normal outlier behavior, which are prior statistical models of normal behaviors, or try building correlations between disperse alerts to recognize a known pattern.[44]

---

[40] "ProjectSauron: top level cyber-espionage platform covertly extracts encrypted government comms", *Kapersky Secure List*, August 8, 2016.

[41] "Once installed, the main ProjectSauron modules start working as 'sleeper cells', displaying no activity of their own and waiting for 'wake-up' commands in the incoming network traffic. This method of operation ensures ProjectSauron's extended persistence on the servers of targeted organizations" (Kapersky Secure List, op. cit.).

[42] "Predictions for 2017: Indicators of compromise are dead", Kapersky Lab annual report, https://kasperskycontenthub.com/securelist/files/2016/11/KL_Predictions_2017.pdf.

[43] http://usa.kaspersky.com/about-us/press-center/press-releases/2016/Clues_are_Dead-Kaspersky_Lab_Researchers_Announce_Threat_Predictions_for_2017.

[44] Cuppens and Miège (2002).

Knowledge-based detection systems, which search for known and legitimate signatures of attacks into monitored events, can also be automated, but automation would typically concerns the automatic triggering of comparison with prior knowledge of signatures, which the learning module would still require from an external and prior teaching.[45]

Such an approach, even when automated, requires regularly updating and distributing a previously acquired knowledge base, while suffering from the inability to detect unknown attacks. Both knowledge-based and behavior-based typically involve creating a centralized database and updating it.

Predictive learning of behavior is critical for a next generation in cyber-security. Future detection technologies will not only detect, but also precisely learns why a machine behavior is incongruous. This learning will be embedded in a local machine, and be accessed only on this local machine (or object, organic component, etc.).

As we have shown in this last section, attackers in the forthcoming years will leave less "symptoms" of their presence. Automated probes and scans, intelligent agents and net centric warfare will become widely share techniques amongst attackers. Hence, attribution will rely on cognitive and behavioral technologies. Most threats will defeat pattern detection, leading discriminative models for pattern in malicious codes to suffer from a lack of "grasp" for their normalization factoring. In other words, lacking patterns will mean focusing on continuous authenticity assessment. As we observed in the several cases discussed in this monograph, such as APT 28, APT 29, the Bangladesh cyber-heist, most contemporary threats are intensively using *contrived incongruity* techniques, i.e. displaying the false appearance of compliance, by matching their dynamic behaviors with targets' expectation. Most recent defensive techniques have used work factor analysis (WFA), cognitive puzzling (morphing networks) to deter intelligent attacks; but the only sustainable defense against contrived incongruity attacks is to nurture singularity, and to equal the behavioral intelligence of defense with the behavioral intelligence of attacks. The following table summarizes our key findings and recommendations for such an emerging paradigm: Table 4.9.

[45] Almgren et al. (2008).

Table 4.9 Required learning strategies for emerging threats

New threats	Characteristics	Required defensive strategies
Asymptomatic threats	Attackers escape IOC detection by leaving less symptoms of their presence	Unsupervised learning that constantly watch and control the internal behavioral consistency of networks (congruity vs. incongruity)
Decreased attribution	Attackers use ephemeral attack vectors with embedded cryptographic and intelligent scripting platforms	Use of artificial intelligence to build machine self-awareness and situational awareness
Congruous and compliant	Artificial intelligence is embedded in attack platforms as to dynamically contrive the congruence and compliance of their operations	Base deterrence policy and strategy as if every threat had the characteristics of an insider threat: legitimate, privileged, knowledgeable, friendly, unnoticeable

References

Al-Jarrah O, Arafat A (2014) Network intrusion detection system using attack behavior classification. In: 5th international conference on Information and communication systems (ICICS), 2014 pp 1–6, 1–3

Almgren M, Lindqvist U, Jonsson E (2008) A multi-sensor model to improve automated attack detection. In: 11th international symposium on recent advances in intrusion detection, RAID

Baumard P (1994) From noticing to making sense: using intelligence to develop strategy. Int J Intell Counterintelligence 7(1)

Bierly PE, Gallagher S, Spender JC (2008) Innovation and learning in high-reliability organizations: a case study of united states and russian nuclear attack submarines, 1970–2000. IEEE Trans Eng manag 55(3):393–408. doi:10.1109/TEM.2008.922643

Bourrier M (1996) Organizing maintenance work at two American nuclear power plants. J Contingencies Crisis Manag 4(2):104–112

Byron RK (2016) Hackers' bid to steal $870 m more from Bangladesh central bank foiled. Asian News

Cheung S, Lindqvist U, Fong MW (2003) Modeling multistep cyber attacks for scenario recognition. In: DARPA information survivability conference and exposition (DISCEX III), Washington, D.C, pp 284–292

Chow CK (1970) On optimum recognition error and reject tradeoff. IEEE Trans Inf Theor IT-16 (1):41–46

Cuppens F, Miège A (2002) Alert correlation in a cooperative intrusion detection framework. In: IEEE symposium on security and privacy

Freud S (1905) Jokes and their relation to the unconscious, (trans: Strachey J). Routledge and Kegan Paul, New York

Fry M, Fischer M, Smith P (2010) Challenge identification for network resilience, 65th EURO-NF conference next generation internet (NGI 10). IEEE Press, pp. 1–8

Garfinkel SL, Dinolt G (2011) Operations with degraded security. IEEE Secur Priv 9(6):43–48

Hansen LK, Liisberg C, Salamon P (1997) The error-reject tradeoff. Open Syst Inf Dyn 4:159–184

Jones RV (1975) The theory of practical joking–an elaboration. Inst Math its Appl 11(2):10–17

Jones RV (1978) Most secret war: british scientific intelligence 1939–1945. Hamish Hamilton, London

Juels A, Yen T-F (2012) Sherlock holmes and the case of the advanced persistent threat. In: 5th USENIX workshop on large-scale exploits and emergent threats (LEET)

Kloft M, Laskov P (2011) Online anomaly detection under adversarial impact. In: JMLR workshop and conference proceedings 9 (AISTATS 2010), 12 May–14 May 2010, Sardinia, Italy.
Kushner D (2013) The real story of stuxnet. IEEE Spectr 50(3):48–53
Langner R (2011) Stuxnet: dissecting a cyberwarfare weapon. Secur Priv IEEE 9(3):49–51
Li F, Lai A (2011) Evidence of advanced persistent threat: a case study of malware for political espionage. In: 6th international conference on malicious and unwanted software proceedings, pp 102–109
Liu S-T, Chen Y-M, Hung H-C (2012) N-Victims: an approach to determine N-victims for APT investigations. In: Information security applications. (Lecture notes in computer science), vol 7690, pp 226-240
Majorczyk F, Totel E, Mé L, (2007) Monitoring a network service without knowing the threats?. RNSA conference proceedings
Markou M, Singh S (2003) Novelty detection: a review—part1: statistical approaches. Sig process 83:2481–2497
Marsland S (2003) Novelty detection in learning systems. Neural comput surv 3(2):157–195
Miller GA, Galanter E, Pribram KH (1960) Plans and the structure of behavior. Holt, Rinehart & Winston, New York
Morreall, J (1987) Funny ha-ha, funny strange, and other reactions to incongruity. In: Morreall J (ed) The philosophy of laughter and humor. State University of New York Press, Albany
Nelson B (2010) Behavior of Machine Learning Algorithms in Adversarial Environments. (PhD dissertation). University of California, Berkeley, Department of EECS technical report UCB/EECS-2010-140. November 23
Olsavsky VL (2005) Implementing a patternless intrusion detection system a methodology for Zippo. Ph Dissertation, Monterey, California. Naval Postgraduate School
Ou, X, Rajagopalan SR, Sakthivelmurugan S (2009) An empirical approach to modeling uncertainty in intrusion analysis.In: 2009 annual computer security applications conference proceedings pp 494–503
Rauterberg M (1995) About a framework for information and information processing of learning systems. In: Proceedings of the IFIP international working conference on information system concepts: towards a consolidation of views. Chapman & Hall, Ltd. London, UK, pp 54–69
Roberts S, Tarassenko L (1994) A probabilistic resource allocating network for novelty detection. Neural Comput 6:270–284
Roschlin GI, Meier AV (1994) Nuclear Power Operations: A Cross-Cultural Perspective.Annu Rev Energ Env 19(1): 153–187
Shultz TR (1972) The role of incongruity and resolution in children's appreciation of jokes and cartoons: an information-processing analysis. J Exp Child Psychol 13:456–477
Sood AK., Enbody R (2012) Targeted cyber attacks—a superset of advanced persistent threats, IEEE Secur Priv 99
Sterbenz JPG et al (2010) Resilience and survivability in communication networks: strategies, principles, and survey of disciplines. Comput Netw 54(8):1245–1265
Virvilis N, Gritzalis D, Apostolopoulos T (2013) Trusted computing vs. advanced persistent threats: can a defender win this game? In: Ubiquitous intelligence and computing, 2013 IEEE 10th international conference on and 10th international conference on autonomic and trusted computing (uic/atc), pp 396–403, 18–21
Yap C, Calonzo A (2016) Printer error foiled billion-dollar bank heist. Sydney Morning Herald
Yeung DY, Ding Y (2002) Host-based intrusion detection using dynamic and static behavioral models. Pattern Recognition 36:229–243

Chapter 5
Conclusion

This monograph explored the national preparedness and performance of France's national cyber security strategy. In our first chapter, we studied the emergence of the "cyber domain" as a worldwide phenomenon towards a more systematic and sovereign practice of computer and network security as a conduit for power and the defense of national interests. We dispute the rise of cognitive warfare (1972–2001) as being a doctrinal continuum for Cold War-inherited perspectives of conventional warfare. This preliminary analysis led to dire conclusions: a dominance of information infrastructure has failed to enforce a pacification of cyberspace. By transporting obsolete conceptions of warfare to cyberspace, early doctrines of cyberwarfare failed to understand the profoundly asymmetric nature of cyber confrontations. The early doctrines of cognitive dominance (2001–2005) pursued these early misconceptions. They led to a global reluctance to adopt and share a communal framework for cyber stability, both on its criminal aspects (Budapest convention) and in defining an adequate model for strategic resolution and de-escalation of cyber conflicts. Policy-makers and crafters of the early doctrines for national cyber-security have misunderstood the deeply dynamic nature of cyberspace; ignoring its autonomous development; its hunger for creativity and freedom of expression; and trying to impose a vertical control over an highly ubiquitous, open and transnational new domain.

When real cyber-confrontations emerged (2006–2016), most countries were unprepared, carrying misleading expertise, obsolete doctrines written by computer-illiterate warmongers, and inspired by political fantasies of a split and aggressive cyberspace. We compared the birth of national cyber security strategies to the *Opposing shore* (*Le rivage des Syrtes*), a novel by French writer Julien Gracq published in 1951. Isolated doctrinal fortresses watched each other from distant shores. Bored by inaction and an ever-lasting silence, old belligerents started to be obsessed with eventual signals of a forthcoming war. A war of hypothetical attributions of cyber attacks, interpreted as national willingness of escalating cyber confrontations into warfare, followed. Indicators of compromise that would have been evidence of foreign adversaries were actively sought. The "Chinese" APT1

P. Baumard, *Cybersecurity in France*, SpringerBriefs in Cybersecurity,
DOI 10.1007/978-3-319-54308-6_5

and the “Russian” Estonian cyber attack were the first historical examples of this *Opposing shore* era.

In the second chapter of this monograph, we attempted to put our analysis of the French national cyber security strategy in its historical grounding. This chapter tries to understand how, over a period of 45 years (1972–2017), the joyful, pioneering and rather innocent practice of *hacking* was transformed into a subject of sovereignty and national interest. As we investigated the early and founding years of hacking, we grouped cyber attacks into four generations, based on their sponsorship (spontaneous vs. sponsored) and their teleology (non-directed vs. targeted). In this chapter, we investigate the emergence of the French cybersecurity and hacking community in the early 1980s, and its transformation into a very active and creative group of young hackers in the mid 1990s (pp. 29–30 and 32–34). The chapter describes an autonomous development of global cybercrime, unrelated to national cyber strategies, and derived from the monetization of cyberspace in the late 1990s. The involvement of nation-States in national cyber-strategies truly emerge in the mid-2000s when actual worldwide cyber campaigns target sovereign institutions: United Nations, US government, Russian and Chinese central commands, etc.

The chapter of this monograph deals with the determinants of a national cyber-security strategy. Purposefully, we did not separate in this section the notions of cybercrime, cyberdefense and enterprise cybersecurity. The objective of this section was to understand the in-depth societal transformation that would ultimately lead to the hybridizing of the three sub-domains. This section introduces a core concept of national cyber-response: the possibility of counter-measures. As we investigate several classes of counter-measures (interdiction, prevention and proactive), we unveil the difficulty of designing a national cyber-security strategy without impeding the foundations of individual freedom, privacy and sovereignty. The findings in this section suggests that the impossibility of conducting sound and non-opposable attribution is stalling and impeding the emergence of shared international framework for cyber-conflict and cyber-crime resolution. In particular, we discuss the Russian position, which has been at the core of the negotiations and the lack of ratification of a communal framework. This chapter was the opportunity to illustrate the mechanisms of a failing attribution with a contemporary case study. Lacking of a significant French case study, we chose to explore the case study of the alleged cyber-attacks on the Democratic National Committee (DNC) during the United States presidential election campaign. We chose this case as to illustrate the difficulties that could be met by the newly proposed French cyber-doctrine of December 12, 2016. The case study as revealing: definite attribution of the cyber attacks was impossible to establish. When we looked into the details of the Indicators of compromise, of the country of origin of the attacks, of the tools being used, it was becoming evident that the overall attack campaign would remain unattributed; at least, with the evidence available in January 2017. We concluded this section by witnessing the dire impact of causal ambiguities on national policies. Non-determinacy, and the incapacity of establishing intentionality from the traces of an attack, made it impossible to transfer an escalation or de-escalation model from traditional defense doctrines.

In this context, we reviewed the specific history of French national doctrines and national strategies for cyber-security. Instead of focusing on organizational charts, division of labor and specialized units, we chose to analyze the cultural and technological determinants that could shape a French national cyber-security strategy. We study in this section the seven national reports and initiatives that progressively shaped the final 2016 "national digital strategy". We concluded this section by highlighting the role of the integration of republican values into the latest evolution of French national digital strategy.

The fourth and last chapter of this monograph deals with the forthcoming strategic shifts of national cyber-doctrines. More precisely, this last chapter explores, in a first section, the differences and similarities between the 35 studied national doctrines, and in a second section, attempts to assess the consequences of forthcoming technological evolutions on a national defense strategy. We did not address these strategic shifts from the sole perspective of the French national case study. It would not make sense to isolate France as a specific expression of these changes. Even if France has demonstrated a strong leadership in artificial intelligence research, participating in some major industry changes such as deep learning, the shifts that we discuss in this last section of the monograph have a much broader impact than its eventual influence on the French national cyber-security strategy. We did not either discuss the eventual strengths or vulnerabilities of the French national infrastructures, education and industry in regard of these changes. Our study suggests, however, that French governmental initiatives in the period 2008–2017 operated a shift from a doctrine that belonged to a "technocratic vision" in 2008, from a national strategy that clearly joined the "pack" of power-sovereign doctrines (along with Russia, China, Germany and the United States) in the early 2017 (see Figs. 4.3 and 4.4).

The concluding section of this monograph is a reflection on our findings. In a more technical approach, yet accessible, we discuss the growing role of artificial intelligence in the new generation of advanced persistent threats (APTs). This section proposes the birth of a "behavioral intelligence" paradigm, where the sole identification and attribution technique lies in being able to recognize the "behavioral DNA" of an attack. As we review the differences between the signature paradigm and the behavioral paradigm, we suggest that normative detection techniques, and thus, normative defense, will likely collapse in the near future. We introduce in this section the use of behavioral intelligence models based on R.V. Jones's elaboration of incongruity, as we draw a parallel between artificial intelligence induced attacks and this threat intelligence framework.

This monograph of "Cybersecurity in France" depicted a cyber-arena in constant evolution. We are entering, communally and inescapably, an era of highly intelligent and automated cyber-threats, with failing attributions, obsolete doctrinal frameworks, and a very dangerous mindset that puts computer illiteracy at the center of over-reactions and uncontrolled escalations. Let's hope that the implicit message of reason, moderation and caution with wrongful attribution, will encourage future policy-makers and the technical community to pursue resilience and cyber-stability with behavioral intelligence at hand, and a willingness to cooperate at heart.

Bibliography

Abrahamson E (1991) Managerial fad and fashion: the diffusion and rejection of innovations. Acad Manag Rev 16(3):586–612

Abrahamson E, Fombrun CJ (1992) Forging the iron cage: interorganizational networks and the production of macro-culture. J Manage Stud 29:175–194

Ah-Pine J, Lemoine J, Benhadda H (2005) Un nouvel outil de classification non supervisée de documents pour la découverte de connaissances et la détection de signaux faibles. Journée sur les systèmes d'information élaborés, Île Rousse

Akoka Jacky (CEDRIC-CNAM), Isabelle Comyn-Wattiau (CEDRIC-CNAM), Cédric Du Mouza (CEDRIC-CNAM), Hammou Fadili Nadira Lammari (CEDRIC-CNAM), Elisabeth Metais (CEDRIC-CNAM) and Samira Si-Said Cherfi (CEDRIC-CNAM) (2014) A semantic approach for semi-automatic detection of sensitive data. Inf Resour Manag J 27(4):23–44

Alchian A (1950) Uncertainty, evolution, and economic theory. J Polit Econ 57:211–221

Amarilli A, Naccache D, Rauzy P, Simion E (2011) Can a program reverse-engineer itself? Cryptography and Coding

ANSSI (2011) Information systems defence and security: France's strategy. National Report

Aoki PM, Honicky RJ, Mainwaring A, Myers C, Paulos E, Subramanian S, Woodruff A (2009) A vehicle for research: using street sweepers to explore the landscape of environmental community action. In: Proceedings of CHI 2009, Boston, MA, April 2009, pp 375–384. Best Paper Nominee

Atkinson SR, Moffat J (2005) The agile organization: from informal networks to complex effects and agility. DoD CCRP Publications, Washington

Badal A (2005) Using interdisciplinary thinking to improve strategy formulation: a managerial perspective. Int J Manag 22(3):365–375

Barreno MBA, Nelson A, Joseph D, Tygar D (2008) The security of machine learning. EECS Department, University of California, Berkeley, Technical report UCB/EECS-2008-43, April 2008

Barreno M, Nelson B, Joseph A, Tygar J (2010) The security of machine learning. Mach Learn 81 (2):121–148

Bartunek JM, Louis MR (1996) Insider/Outsider team research. Qualitative research methods, vol 40. Sage, Thousand Oaks, CA

Bauer et al (2008) Déceler, étudier, former: une voie nouvelle pour la recherche stratégique. Rapport au Président de la République et au Premier Ministre

Baumard P (1996) From infowar to knowledge warfare: preparing for the paradigm shift. In: Campen A, Dearth D, Gooden R (eds) Cyberwar: security, strategy and conflict in the information age. Armed Forces Communications and Electronics Association, International Press, Fairfax, Virginia, pp 147–160

Baumard P (1999) Tacit knowledge in organizations. Sage, London

Baumard Ph (2008) Using machine foreknowledge to enhance human cognition. In: Naim P, Pourret O, Marcot BG (eds) Bayesian belief networks: a practical guide to applications. Wiley, New York, pp 365–375

Bea R (2006) Reliability and human factors in geotechnical engineering. J Geotech Geoenviron Eng 132(5):631

Benghozi P-J, Paris T (2005) The distribution function: at the heart of managing cultural-product industries. In: Best paper proceedings, 8th international conference on arts at cultural management. Montréal, Canada

Bengtsson M, Kock S (2000) Co-opetition in business networks, to cooperate and compete simultaneously. Ind Market Manag 19(5):411–426

Bigley GA, Roberts KH (2001) The incident command system: high-reliability organizing for complex and volatile task environments. Acad Manag J 44(6):1281–1299

Bodmer S, Kilger M, Carpenter G, Jones J (2012) Reverse deception: organized cyber threat counter-exploitation. McGraw-Hill Osborne Media, New York

Brandenburger AM, Nalebuff J (1996) Co-opetition. Harvard business school, Boston
Brooks RA (1997) From earwigs to humans. Robot Auton Syst 20(2–4):291–304
Burger J, Brill D, Machi F (1980) Self-reproducing programs. Byte 5:74–75
Bürki-Cohen J (2008) Literature for flight simulator (motion) requirements research. U.S. Department of Transportation, Federal Aviation Administration, Washington, DC
Bürki-Cohen J, Sparko AL (2008) Airplane upset prevention research needs. In: Proceedings of the AIAA modeling and simulation technologies conference, 18–21 Aug 2008, Honolulu, HI, AIAA 2008–6871
Burt RS (1992) The social structure of competition. Harvard Business School Press, Cambridge
Cheng J, Greiner R (1999) Comparing Bayesian network classifiers. In: Proceedings of the 15th international conference on uncertainty in artificial intelligence, Stockholm, Sweden
Chow C, Liu C (1968) Approximating discrete probability distributions with dependence trees. IEEE Trans Inf Theory 14(3):462–467
Cooper G, Herskovits E (1992) A Bayesian method for the induction of probabilistic networks from data. Mach Learn 9(4):309–347
Deepayan C (2004) Autopart: Parameter-free graph partitioning and outlier detection. In: PKDD, pp 112–124
Depeyre C, Dumez H (2007) Le rôle du client dans les stratégies de coopétition: le cas de l'industrie américaine de défense. Revue Française de Gestion 33(176)
Depeyre C, Dumez H (2009) A management perspective on market dynamics: stabilizing and destabilizing strategies in the US defense industry. Eur Manag J 27(2):90–99
Derks PL, Gillikin LS (1993) Incongruity, incongruity resolution and mental states: the measure and modification of situational awareness and control. In: Final Report, NASA Research Grant NCC1-160, Unclassified Document (July 1993)
Donald SD, McMillen RV, Ford DK, McEachen JC (2002) Therminator 2: a thermodynamics-based method for real-time patternless intrusion detection. In: Proceedings MILCOM 2002, vol. 2, pp 1498, 1502 vol. 2, pp 7–10 (Oct 2002)
Druzdzel MJ, Simon HA (1993) Causality in bayesian belief networks. In: Proceedings of the ninth annual conference on uncertainty in artificial intelligence, San Francisco, CA, San Mateo: Morgan Kaufmann Publishers, pp 3–11
Druzdzel MJ, Van Leijen H (2001) Causal reversibility in Bayesian networks. J Exp Theor Artif Intell 13(1):45–62
Dua S, Xian D (2011) Data Mining and Machine Learning in Cybersecurity. Taylor & Francis Publishing—CRC Press, Boca Raton, FL
Dumez H (2005) Comprendre l'innovation: le chaînon manquant. Gérer and Comprendre, No 81:66–73
Endsley MR (1997) The role of situation awareness in naturalistic decision-making. In: Zsambok C (eds) Naturalistic decision-making. Erlbaum, Mahwah, NJ, pp 269–284
Eskin E, Arnold A, Prerau M, Portnoy L, Stolfo S (2002) A geometric framework for unsupervised anomaly detection: detecting intrusions in unlabeled data. In: Jajodia S, Barbara D (eds) Applications of data mining in computer security, Chap. 4. Kluwer, Dordrecht
Feng C, Ri T, Yi Z, Jinshu S (2009) Two scalable analyses of compact attack graphs for defending network security. In: Networks security, wireless communications and trusted computing, 2009. NSWCTC '09. International Conference on, vol. 1, pp. 627, 632, 25–26 (IEEE Apr 2009)
Ferrier WJ, Smith KG, Grimm CM (1999) The rôle of compétitive action in market share érosion and industry dethronment: A study of industry leaders and challengers. Acad Manag J 42: 372–383
Fogla P, Lee W (2006) Evading network anomaly detection systems: Formal reasoning and practical techniques In: Proceedings of the 13th ACM conference on computer and communications security, CCS '06. New York, NY, USA. ACM, pp 59–68
Freudenthal D (2001) The role of age, foreknowledge and complexity in learning to operate a complex device. Behav Inf Technol 20(1):23–135
Friedman N, Geiger D, Goldszmidt M (1997) Bayesian network classifiers. Mach Learn 29:131–163

Fritz J (1975) Distribution-free exponential error bound for nearest neighbor pattern classification. IEEE Trans. Inform. Theory 21:552–557

Garcia J, Koelling RA (1966) Relationship of cue to consequence in avoidance learning. Psychon Sci 4:123–124

Gavetti GG, Levinthal DD (2000) Looking forward and looking backward: cognitive and experiential search. Adm Sci Q 45(1):113–137

Gaycken S (2012) Die sieben Plagen des Cyberwar. In: Schmidt-Radefeldt R, Meissler C (eds) Automatisierung und Digitalisierung des Krieges. Forum Innere Führung, Berlin

Ghosh D, Sharman R, Rao H, Upadhyaya S (2007) Self-healing systems: survey and synthesis. Decis Support Syst 42:2164–2185

Girvan M, Newman MEJ (2002) Community structure in social and biological networks. In: Proc. Natl. Acad. Sci., vol. 99, USA

Goerzen A, Beamish P (2005) The effect of alliance network diversity on multinational enterprise performance. Strateg Manag J 26(4):333–354

Graf P, Schacter DL (1985) Implicit and explicit memory for new associations in normal and amnesic subjects. J Exp Psychol Learn Mem Cogn 11:501–518

Granovetter MS (1973) The strength of weak ties. Am J Sociol 78:1360–1380

Hamrefors S (1999) Spontaneous environmental scanning: putting the 'putting into perspective' into perspective. Ph.D. dissertation, Stockholm School of Economics

Haizhi X, Du W, Chapin SJ (2004) Context sensitive anomaly monitoring of process control flow to detect mimicry attacks and impossible paths. Recent Adv Intrus Detect, Lect Notes Comput Sci 3224(2004):21–38

Hasher L, Zacks RT (1984) Automatic processing of fundamental information. Am Psychol 48:1372–1388

Hedberg B (1981) How organizations learn and unlearn. In: Nystrom P, Starbuck W (eds) Handbook of organizational design. Oxford University Press, New York, pp 1–27

Henderson RM, Clark KB (1990) Architectural innovation: the reconfiguration of existing product technologies and the failure of established firms. Adm Sci Q 35:9–30

Hildebrand K, Smith S (2013) Attentional biases toward humor: separate effects of incongruity detection and resolution. Motivation and Emotion, pp 1–10

Hirsch F (1977) Social limits to growth. Routledge & Kegan Paul, London

James C, Britz J, Vuilleumier P, Hauert C-A, Michel C (2008) Early neuronal responses in right limbic structures mediate harmony incongruity processing in musical experts. NeuroImage 42(4): 1597–1608

Jones RV (1975, jan-fév) The theory of practical joking: an elaboration. The bulletin of the Institute of Mathematics and its Applications, janvier février, pp 10–17

Jones RV (1956) Scientific intelligence. Research 9:347–352

Jones RV (1975) The theory of practical joking—an elaboration. J Inst Math Appl, Jan/Feb, pp 10–17

Journé B, Raulet-Croset N (2008) Le concept de situation: contribution à l'analyse de l'activité managériale dans un contexte d'ambiguïté et d'incertitude. Management 11(1):27–55

Kao J, Levy R, Goodman N (2011) The funny thing about incongruity: a computational model of humor in puns. stanford.edu, 1

Kapoor A, Horvitz E (2007) Principles of lifelong learning for predictive user modelling. In: Proceedings of the eleventh conference on user modelling, June 2007, Corfu, Greece

Kay J, McKiernan P, Faulkner DO (2003) The history of strategy and some thoughts about the future. In: Faulkner DO, Campbell A (eds) The handbook of strategy. Oxford University Press, Oxford, NY

Kearns M, Ming L (1993) Learning in the presence of malicious errors. SIAM J Comput 22(4): 807–837

Kieras DE, Bovair S (1984) The role of a mental model in learning to operate a device. Cogn Sci 8:255–273

Humphrey TE, Ledvina BM, Psiaki ML, O'Hanlon BW, Kintner Jr, PM (2008) Assessing the spoofing threat: development of a portable GPS civilian spoofer. In: Proceedings of the Institute of navigation GNSS conference, Savannah, GA Sept 2008

Koller D, Friedman N (2009) Probabilistic graphical models: principles and techniques. MIT press

Kolodgy CJ (2011) Worldwide security and vulnerability management 2011–2015 Forecast and 2010 Vendor Shares, IDC Research

Konrad AB, Zhao Y, Joseph AD (2006) Determining model accuracy of network traces. J. Comput Syst Sci: Perform Model Eval Comput Syst 72(7):1156–1171

Lado AG, Boyd NG, Hanlon SC (1997) Competition, cooperation and the search for economic rents: a syncretic model. Acad Manag Rev 22(1):110–141

Lakhina AMC, Christophe D (2005) Detecting distributed attacks using network-wide flow traffic. In: Proceedings of the FloCon 2005 analysis workshop

Lampson BW (1973) A note on the confinement problem, Xerox Palo Alto Research Center

Langer E, Blank A, Chanowitz B (1978) The mindlessness of ostensibly thoughtful action: the role of 'placebic' information in interpersonal interaction. J Pers Soc Psychol 36:635–642

Lankveld G, Spronck P, Herik H, Rauterberg M (2010) Incongruity-based adaptive game balancing. In: Herik H, Spronck P (eds) Advances in computer games, vol 6048., Lecture notes in computer scienceBerlin Heidelberg, Springer, pp 208–220

Laskov P, Lippmann R (2010) Machine learning in adversarial environments. Mach Learn 81 (2):115–119

Lenfle S, Midler C (2009) The launch of innovative product-related services: lessons from automotive telematics. Res Policy 38(1):156–169

Lessig L (2007) Does copyright have limits? Eldred v. Ashcroft and its aftermath. In: Fitzgerald B (ed) Open content licensing: cultivating the creative commons. Sydney University Press, Sydney

Lewicki P (1986) Non conscious social information processing. Academic Press, New York

Lin T, Xiaolan Z, Xiao M, Weiwei X, Yuanyuan Z (2008) AutoISES: automatically inferring security specifications and detecting violations. In: Proceedings of the 17th conference on Security symposium, July 28-August 01, San Jose, CA, pp 379–394

Ling H, Joseph AD, Blaine N, Rubinstein BIP, Tygar JD (2011) Adversarial Machine Learning. In: Proceedings of the 4th ACM workshop on artificial intelligence and security, ACM, 21 Oct 2011

Lo SC, Peterson BB, Enge PK (2009) Assessing the security of a navigation system: a case study using enhanced loran. In: Proceedings of the Institute of Navigation GNSS Conference

M'chirgui Z (2005) The economics of the smart card industry: towards coopetitive strategies. Econ Innov New Technol 14(6):455–477

Mahmoud-Jouini BS, Charue-Duboc F (2008) Enhancing discontinuous innovation though knowledge combination: the case of an exploratory unit within an established automotive firm. Creativity Innov Manag 17(2):127–135

Mahoney MV, Chan PK (2002) Learning non stationary models of normal network traffic for detecting novel attacks. Proceedings of the 8th ACM SIGKDD international conference on knowledge discovery and data mining (KDD). ACM Press, New York, pp 376–385

Majorczyk FET, Ludovic M, Ayda S (2007) Détection d'intrusions et diagnostic d'anomalies dans un système diversifié par comparison de graphes de flux d'information. In: proceedings of the 2nd conference on security in network architectures and information systems (SAR-SSI'2007). June 2007

Manqi Z, Venkatesh S (2009) Anomaly detection with score functions based on nearest neighbor graphs. In: Bengio Y, Schuurmans D, Lafferty J, Williams CKI, Culotta A (eds) Advances in neural information processing systems, 22, pp 2250–2258

Marco B, Bartlett PL, Chi FJ, Joseph AD, Nelson B, Rubinstein BI, Saini U, Tygar JD (2008) Open problems in the security of learning. In: First acm workshop on security and artificial intelligence (AISec), Alexandria, Virginia, pp 19–26

Marco B, Bartlett PL, Chi FJ, Joseph AD, Nelson B, Rubinstein BIP, Saini U, Tygar JD (2008) Open problems in the security of learning. In: The proceedings of the first ACM workshop on AISec, pp 19–26

Markou M, Sameer S (2003) Novelty detection: a review—part 2: neural network based approaches. Sig Process 83(12):2499–2521

McEachen JC, Cheng KW, Olsavsky VL (2006) Aggregating distributed sensor data for network intrusion detection. In: 11th IEEE symposium on computers and communications, pp 916–922

Meyer TA, Whateley B (2004) Spambayes: effective open-source, bayesian based, email classification system. In: CEAS. Citeseer

Modelo-Howard G, Saurabh B, Guy L (2008) Determining placement of intrusion detectors for a distributed application through bayesian network modeling. In: 11th international symposium on recent advances in intrusion detection (RAID 2008). RAID, Sep 2008

Monge P, Contractor N (2003) Theories of communication networks. Oxford University Press, USA, p 432

Mylavarapu S, Walch S, Marinovich J, Zachary J, McEachen J, Ford D (2004) Monitoring conversation exchange dynamics for detection of epidemic-style computer network attacks

Nelson B, Rubinstein BIP, Ling H, Joseph AD, Tygar JD (2011) Classifier Evasion: Models and Open Problems, In Privacy and Security Issues. In: Data Mining and Machine Learning, volume 6549 of Lecture Notes in Computer Science, pp 92–98

Newsome J, Karp B, Song D (2005) Polygraph: automatically generating signatures for polymorphic worms. In: Security and privacy, 2005 IEEE symposium on, pp 226–241

Newsome J, Brad K, Dawn S (2006) Paragraph: thwarting signature learning by training maliciously. In: Proceedings of the 9th international symposium on recent advances in intrusion detection, September 2006

Nguyen LH, Joseph AD (2008) Support vector machines, data reduction, and approximate kernel matrices. In: Daelemans W, Goethals B, Morik K (eds) Machine learning and knowledge discovery in databases—part II: Proc. European conf. (ECML/PKDD 2008), Lecture notes in computer science: lecture notes in artificial intelligence, Vol. 5212, Berlin, Germany: Springer, pp 137–153

Nooteboom B, Gilsing VA (2004) Density and strength of ties in innovation networks: a competence and governance view. In: Erim report series research in management, No ERS-2004-005-ORG

Oman CM, Kendra AJ, Hayashi M, Stearns MD, Bürki-Cohen J Vertical navigation displays: pilot performance and workload during simulated constant-angle-of-descent GPS approaches. Int J Aviat Psychol 11(1):15–31

Paxson V (1999) Bro: A system for detecting network intruders in real-time. Comput Netw 31(23): 2435–2463

Pearl J (1995) Causal diagrams for empirical research. Biometrika 82:669–710

Perrow C (1984) Normal accidents: living with high-risk technologies. Princeton University Press, p 451

Philips A (1960) A theory of interfirm organization. Quart J Econ 74:602–613

Polanyi M (1966) The tacit dimension. Routledge, London, and University of Chicago Press, Chicago

Rauterberg M (1993) Amme: an automatic mental model evaluation to analyze user behaviour traced in a finite, discrete state space. Ergonomics 36(11):1369–1380

Rauterberg M (1994) About the relationship between incongruity, complexity and information: design implications for man-machine systems. In: Rauch W, Strohmeier F, Hiller H, Schlögl C (eds) Mehrwert von Information–Professionalisierung der Informationsarbeit. Konstanz: Universitätsverlag, pp 122–132

Reber AS (1993) Implicit learning and tacit knowledge: an essay on the cognitive unconscious. Oxford psychology series no. 19. Oxford University Press, Oxford

Roberts KH, Stout SK, Halpern JJ (1994) Decision dynamics in two high reliability military organizations. Manage Sci 40(5):614–624

Rochlin GI, Meier AV (1994) Nuclear power operations: a cross-cultural perspective. Annu Rev Energy Env 19(1):153–187
Rouvroy A (2008) Réinventer l'art d'oublier et de se faire oublier dans la société de l'information?, La sécurité de l'individu numérisé. Réflexions prospectives et internationales
Rouvroy A (2009) Governmentality in an age of autonomic computing. technology, virtuality and Utopia. Autonomic computing and transformations of human agency. Philosophers of Law meet Philosophers of Technology
Rubinstein BIP, Blaine N, Ling H, Joseph AD, Shing-hon L, Satish R, Nina T, Tygar JD (2009) ANTIDOTE: understanding and defending against poisoning of anomaly detectors. In: IMC'09: proceedings of the 9th acm sigcomm on internet measurement conference, Chicago, IL, pp 1–14
Sakthivelmurugan S (2009) An empirical approach to modeling uncertainty in intrusion analysis. Master of Science Dissertation, Kansas State University, Manhattan, Kansas, 2009
Samson A (2008) Cognitive and neural humor processing: the influence of structural stimulus properties and theory of mind
Scott L (2003) Anti-spoofing and authenticated signal architectures for civil navigation systems. In: Proceedings of the institute of navigation GPS conference, Portland OR, Sept 2003
Segal R, Crawford J, Kephart JO, Leiba B (2004) Spamguru: an enterprise anti-spam filtering system. In: CEAS
Shannon C (1948) A mathematical theory of communication. Bell Syst Tech J 27:379–390
Silberzhan P, Midler C (2008) Creating Products in the Absence of Markets: A Robust Design Approach. Journal of Manufacturing Technology Management 19(3):407–420
Simon HA (1962) The architecture of complexity. Proc Am philos soc 106(2):467–482
Singaravelu L et al (2006) Reducing TCB complexity for security-sensitive applications: three case studies. In: Eurosys '06, Apr 18–21
Spirtes P, Glymour C, Scheines R (1993) Causation, prediction, and search. Springer, New York
Starbuck WH (1981) A trip to view the elephants and rattlesnakes in the garden of Aston. In: Van de Ven AH, Joyce WF (eds) Perspectives on organization design and behavior. Wiley, pp 167–198
Starbuck WH (1992) Strategizing in the real world. In: international journal of technology management, special publication on technological foundations of strategic management, vol. 8, nos. 1/2
Starbuck WH (1995) "How Organizations Channel Creativity", in C. M. Ford and D. A. Gioia (eds.), *Creative Action in Organizations*; Sage, 1995, pages 106–114
Starbuck WH (1996) Unlearning ineffective or obsolete technologies. Int J Technol Manag 11:725–737
Starbuck WH, Milliken FJ (1988) Challenger: Fine-tuning the odds until something breaks. J Manage Stud 25:319–340
Starbuck WH, Barnett ML, Baumard P (2008) Payoffs and pitfalls of strategic learning. J Econ Behav Organ 66(1):7–21
Stibor T, Mohr P, Timmis J (2005) Is negative selection appropriate for anomaly detection? In: GECCO '05 proceedings of the 2005 conference on genetic and evolutionary computation, pp 321–328
Stolfo S, Hershkop S, Wang K, Nimeskern O, Hu C-W (2003) A behavior-based approach to securing email systems. In: Gorodetsky V, Popyack L, Skormin V (eds) Computer network security, vol 2776., Lecture Notes in Computer ScienceSpringer, Berlin Heidelberg, pp 57–81
Stolfo SJ, Li W-J, Hershkop S, Wang K, Hu C-W, Nimeskern O (2004) Detecting viral propagations using email behavior profiles. In: ACM transactions on internet technology (TOIT), pp 128–132
Suchier JM, Blancher C, Bruguiere JL, Deswarte Y, Duccoroy JM, Hotte D, Huyghe , de Lastours S, Martini H, de Maupeou S, Mé L, Pochon JP et al. (2012) Contemporary threats and information technologies, new criminalities. In: Report of the scientific council of the high council for strategic education and research (CSFRS), Paris: CNRS Editions, pp 45–52

Tabia K, Salem B, Philippe L, Ludovic M (2011) Alert correlation in intrusion detection: combining AI-based approaches for exploiting security operators' knowledge and preferences. Association for the advancement of artificial intelligence
Tahboub KA (2006) Intelligent human-machine interaction based on dynamic bayesian networks probabilistic intention recognition. J Intell Rob Syst 45(1):31–52
Tkalac S (2000) The types of incongruity and Paulos's model. J Inf Organ Sci 24(1):83–91
Van Lankveld G, Spronck P, Rauterberg M (2008) Difficulty scaling through incongruity. In: Mateas M, Darken C (eds) Proceedings of the fourth artificial intelligence and interactive digital entertainment conference. AAAI Press, pp 228–229
Von Weizsäcker E (1974) Erstmaligkeit und Bestätigung als Komponenten der pragmati-schen Information. In: von Weizsäcker E (ed) Offene Systeme, Band I. Beiträge zur Zeitstruktur von Information, Entropie und Evolution. Klett
Waldman DE, Jensen EJ (2001) Industriel organization. Addison-Wesley, Boston
Webb E, Weick KE (1979) Unobtrusive measures in organizational theory: a reminder. Adm Sci Q 24:650–659
Weick KE (1979) The social psychology of organizing. Addison-Wesley Pub. Co, p 294
Weick KE (1988) Enacted sensemaking in crisis situations. J Manage Stud 25(4):305–317
Weick KE (1995) Sensemaking in organizations, vol 38. Sage Publications Inc., Thousand Oaks, California, p 237
Welles O (1973) F for Fake, documentary, Janus Film
Whaley B (1982) Towards a general theory of deception. In: Gooch John, Perlmutter Amos (eds) Military deception and strategic surprise. Frank Cass & Co, Totowa, NJ
Willingham DB, Preuss L (1995) The death of implicit memory. Psyche 2(15)
Zhai Y, Ning P, Iyer P, Reeves DS (2004) Reasoning about complementary intrusion evidence. In: Proceedings of 20th annual computer security applications conference (ACSAC), Dec 2004, pp 39–48

Kolibri 360 GmbH
Ferdinand-Jühlke-Straße 7
99095 Erfurt, Deutschland
produktsicherheit@kolibri360.de